Understanding Yourself *and* Others

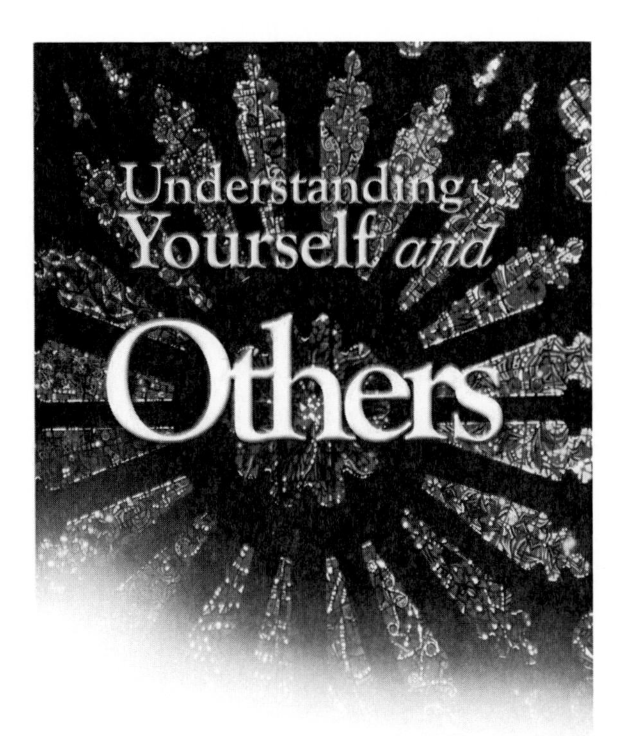

Contributors:

Paul Conn, Ph.D.
Robert W. Fisher, Ph.D.
Doyle Goff, Ph.D.
Jerome Hammond, Ph.D.

Edited by Donald S. Aultman, Ed.D.

Church of God School of Ministry
Cleveland, Tennessee

Scripture passages, unless otherwise noted are from the King James Version of the Holy Bible.

Scripture passages marked *NIV* are from the *Holy Bible, New International Version* ®. *NIV* ®. Copyright © 1973, 1978, 1984 by International Bible Society. Used by permission of Zondervan Publishing House. All rights reserved.

Scripture quotations marked *NKJV* are from the *New King James Version.* Copyright © 1979, 1980, 1982, 1990, 1995, Thomas Nelson Inc., Publishers.

Paul L. Walker, Ph.D.
Chancellor, Division of Education

Donald S. Aultman, Ed.D.
Vice Chancellor, Division of Education
International Director, School of Ministry

Homer G. Rhea, L.H.D.
Editorial Director

ISBN: 978-0-87148-641-7

Copyright © 2001 by Church of God School of Ministry
Cleveland, Tennessee 37311
All Rights Reserved

Printed by Pathway Press
Cleveland, Tennessee

CONTENTS

FOREWORD

When the Lee College Curriculum Committee and faculty were presented proposals in 1969 to offer a major in psychology, two arguments against the idea emerged. Both were valid and needed to be addressed. The first was, How would a major in psychology fulfill the mission of a Christian liberal arts college? The second concern was enrollment. Who would want an undergraduate psychology degree, since only individuals with a master's degree in psychology were employable in the field. After some discussion, the Curriculum Committee and faculty initiated the major in psychology. As the vice president and dean of the college, I was a major proponent of the proposal. The major in psychology soon had one of the largest enrollments in the college. Psychology has appeal because understanding oneself and others is always intriguing.

The first full-time psychology professor who was employed to form the foundation for the department is now the highly acclaimed president of Lee University. Paul Conn came to Lee College as a part-time faculty member shortly after receiving his doctorate (Ph.D.) from Emory University. After designing the psychology major, he joined James L. Slay and me as the initial professors for the psychology major. As a psychology professor for many years, Conn influenced the psychology faculty at Lee, both through his teaching and through faculty acquisitions. As the lead professor in the video course that is the basis for this book, he is joined by three other members from the Lee University psychology faculty: Robert Fisher, Ph.D., Doyle Goff, Ph.D., and Jerome Hammond, Ph.D.

The field of psychology has slowly dropped some of its barriers to the positive treatment of religion and faith—at least in some counseling and mental health systems. As more people of faith, such as Conn, have dedicated their lives to the understanding of the integration of psychology and faith, the church, likewise, has become more open to truth discovered from psychological inquiry that could inform one's faith. Today, a robust discipline is emerging with a growing body of research and literature exploring the integration of psychology and personal religious beliefs. Over the last 30 years, the work of Narramore, Collins, Crabb, Benner, Tan, Moon, and others has created a new era in the integration of psychology and faith. The subjects, so adroitly addressed in this small volume by these dedicated believers from the Lee University psychology faculty, present another example of the direction that Christians are moving the dialogue with some of the concerns of psychology.

Donald S. Aultman, Ed.D.
Vice Chancellor, Division of Education
International Director, School of Ministry

July 2001

PREFACE

Anyone involved in Christian ministry is in the people business. Understanding people is at the heart of effective ministry. To learn the various stages of human existence and to discern where individuals are in their development gives one a decided advantage in ministry.

Believers are not exempt from the common problems that beset humankind. Just because they have accepted Christ does not mean that they will not face conflicts or struggle with their places in society or need to find personal fulfillment in their lives and work. All the dynamics of relationships and family unity impact them as they do others. For a Christian to understand what is happening and how to cope with it is essential to a purposeful and happy life.

Situations of this nature are dealt with in Understanding Yourself and Others. This book offers practical guidance in day-to-day living. It also provides suggestions on how to help others as they face triumphs and tragedies in their lives.

Understanding Yourself and Others is based on a video series bearing the same name. Its greatest value will come from reading it in conjunction with the videotapes. It is offered as part of the Certificate In Ministerial Studies (CIMS) program originated by the School of Ministry.

The contributors to this volume are all actively involved in ministry. At the time of this writing, Dr. Paul Conn serves as president of Lee University in Cleveland, Tennessee; Dr. Robert W. Fisher serves as associate professor of psychology, Dr. Doyle Goff serves as professor of psychology and the director of graduate studies in counseling psychology; and Dr. Jerome Hammond serves as an assistant professor in human development at Lee University.

Several people have been involved in bringing this project to a successful completion. At Media Resource Group (MRG), Wayne Hall and Barry Melton have enthusiastically worked with the School of Ministry from the outset of this endeavor. Abigail Hughes had the arduous task of transcribing the videotapes so they could put them into book form. Dr. Donald S. Aultman's knowledge in the field of psychology was most helpful in editing this book. No one was more valuable to this project than Nellie Keasling who copyedited the manuscript. Sam McGraner is responsi- ble for giving this volume its attractive look, since he designed the cover, flowed the copy, and formatted the book. Jerry Puckett and the staff at Pathway Press are responsible for the printing of this material. This entire project is the brainchild of Dr. Paul L. Walker who has given it his wholehearted support. To each of these, I extend my deepest appreciation and acknowledge that this project would not have been possible without their assistance.

The School of Ministry offers this volume in the hope that it will enhance the ministry of those who read its pages and learn from the lessons it sets forth. May they also gain insight into what makes humankind tick and thereby play a more effective role in advancing the kingdom of God.

Homer G. Rhea, L.H.D.
Editorial Director
School of Ministry
Cleveland, Tennessee
July 2001

1 INTRODUCTION TO UNDERSTANDING YOURSELF AND OTHERS

By Paul Conn, Ph.D.

Every minister needs to become aware of the divine/human equation of ministry, because effective ministry engages all those ways in which the work of God is applied to the condition of man. This involves the communication of God's message to man, as well as the communication of God's grace to man's need. Ministry stands in that gap between all of the great resources and works of God, and the tremendous needs of man. There are two parts to this equation: the God part and the man part. God is the source of all human need, and the individual is the recipient of God's grace and love. The minister stands in the gap between God and man. In all the different ways in which he ministers, he has the same basic task, that is, to reach out to men and women who come into his life and point them to Jesus Christ, the mediator of the resources of God. **Equation: God ⇨ Minister ⇨ Man**

Theology and Ministry

The study of God is, of course, called theology. Theology points to the God side of the ministry equation. Providentially, God reveals Himself to humankind, because otherwise they would never have an understanding of Him. One of the great problems of liberal theology is that it attempts to understand God simply through the operation of logic, reason, and intelligence. God does not require men to find out about Him that way. For someone who truly believes in God, theology is a study of the ways in which God has revealed Himself through the written Word, through the incarnate Word, Jesus Christ, and through the daily work of the Holy Spirit. The study of all these wonderful expressions of God to humanity is called theology.

Mankind and Ministry

In ministry, there is that other part of the equation. In addition to God, who is known through His Word and through His Spirit, there is mankind—the object of all God's work in this world. God loved mankind so much that He gave Himself in the person of the Son (see John 3:16). That is the core of the gospel. All of ministry, in one way or another, involves not just an understanding of God, but an understanding of mankind at every age of development.

The Minister and Ministry

The third part of the ministry equation is the minister standing in the middle. Even though ministers are part of the human family, the better they understand themselves, the more insight they have into what makes them feel, think, and worship the way they do and the greater opportunity they have of standing in the gap between God and man. That is why it is important, not just to understand Scripture and theology, but also to have some insight into this human creature about whom God has so much to say and for whom Jesus Christ came to save. It is important for those who are studying to be ministers to understand themselves and others, as this course title suggests, and to talk about the human organism as they prepare for ministry.

Psychology and Ministry

This study of the human experience is primarily a study of behavioral science—looking at psychology to gain a more adequate understanding of the lives of the people one serves. The word psychology has a negative connotation to many conservative Evangelical Christians. For many years, it has been a misunderstood discipline in the Christian college and university experience. It is not uncommon to find people who still think of psychology as being somehow inherently liberal and hostile to the Word of God or to the simple faith of Scripture. This is not a true view of psychology as a discipline.

> An example of the way in which psychology is often viewed comes out of my own experience: I graduated from Lee College with a degree in theology. But as a minister, I wanted to study psychology at the graduate level to understand more about the people to whom I would minister and to be the most effective minister I could be. With a theology degree, a rich history of God's revelation to His family, and a rich church heritage, I decided to seek additional preparation for ministry by enrolling in a university to study psychology. I wanted

to know more about myself and others. While attending Emory University in Atlanta and studying psychology in a highly respected, but extremely liberal environment, I was simultaneously a youth minister at the Mount Paran Church of God. I began to see very early in my own life how extremely important an adequate understanding of the human experience can be to ministry. I had been discouraged from pursuing this course of study by well-meaning people in my home church. I vividly recall one dear lady, in my home church at North Cleveland, who gave me this kind of advice. She was a very kind lady who first congratulated me then expressed her concern. She said, "Son, don't go down there and let those psychology professors destroy your faith in God." And, you know, she meant that, and I took her words to heart. I was determined not to let those psychology professors destroy my faith in God. I have heard some version of that message for many years since that, right up to the present time. I still teach a psychology class—Understanding Human Behavior—to students here at Lee University every year. The reason I teach them, even though I have a full schedule as the president, is because I consider it to be so very important for them to understand that the human organism is God's grandest creature. The human being is the crown of God's creative genius. When He looked about Him, He saw the sun, the stars, the moon, the earth, the sea, the sky, the beast of the field, and the fowl of the air. With all this creative work complete, He then created His masterpiece—the human organism. Even though man is made of the dust of the earth and is therefore finite and mortal, God declares that he is "fearfully and wonderfully made" (Psalm139:14).

But What Is Psychology?

What then is psychology, and why should one fear that it will destroy his faith in God? Psychology is, in fact, the study of something. When *ology* is placed on the end of any word, it means the study of that subject. For example, geology is the study of the formation of the earth; theology is the study of God; and psychology is the study of the human organism. It is not witchcraft or a set of techniques or a bag of tricks. It is not some system for manipulating someone's behavior. It is the study of human behavior.

The human organism is the handiwork of God—God's creation. The apostle Paul wrote: "For we are God's workmanship, created in Christ Jesus to do good works, which God prepared in advance for us to do" (Ephesians 2:10 NIV). In spite of the quirks, flaws, and mysteries that surround human beings, mankind is God's special project. To study something which God has made cannot be in and of itself wrong. To study that subject properly and with the right presumptions, is to magnify the wonderful works of God.

A tree was made by God. But if one worships trees, and if one thinks that somehow trees spontaneously created themselves out of the earth, the dirt, and the sky, this might lead to some sort of strange and weird approach to life, which would, in fact, inflate the value of trees out of proportion to their actual importance. It would be preposterous to think that studying trees would destroy faith in God. One has no trouble understanding that a tree is just something God made. He created the earth with everything in it, on it, and above it, and a tree was part of it. Likewise, the flowers are part of His creation. There is no concern that flowers will be studied too closely or that botany professors will destroy faith in God. Similarly, psychology is the study of the human organism and its behavior. Where are humans to be led astray in that study? Only in this: if they forget that the human organism was made by God, created and fashioned by God, and that every part of the human experience is a part of God's handiwork. If they analyze this being which God has made, they, in fact, come closer to a full appreciation of just how great God really is.

The experience of driving through and viewing the grandeur of the West, traveling across the ridgetops of the Southern mountains, or riding along the coast in Florida is an awe-inspiring experience. Looking at those vast landscapes, one can sense the greatness of God. It's a cliche to say that nature brings people closer to God because it reminds them of the wonders of the Creator. The study of human behavior can elicit a similar response from the committed Christian. This complex, fascinating organism called a human being comes from Him and belongs to Him. In that context, psychology—the study of the human experience—is not something that denigrates the role of God in the life of mankind. On the contrary, God is elevated as one is reminded over and over again of how great He is.

> That is exactly the experience I had in graduate school studying psychology. And that is the experience I have seen many students have here at Lee University as they get into the study of human behavior and they gradually relinquish the idea that this is about manipulation, ulterior motives, or some sort of vague,

strange subconscious stuff. They learn to relax and understand that psychology is the study of human behavior, and that human behavior comes from God's finest moment of Creation.

The Role of the Minister

A minister studies human behavior to communicate more effectively, because a message is not really useful unless it is heard and understood. People who do not act on what they hear are no better off than those who have not heard. It is not the role of the minister to shout the gospel out into the air. That achieves nothing. His job is to make sure the gospel of Jesus Christ is absorbed and assimilated, resulting in life-changing experiences. The Bible speaks in terms of people eating the meat of the Word (see Hebrews 5:12-14) which leads to growth and change. Whatever form of ministry one enters, its object is to bring about change in human behavior.

Ministry Outcomes

What then is the outcome of ministry? The out- come of worship is to send praise and worship back to God. The outcome of personal piety in devotion is to sense a closeness to God. The outcome of Bible reading is to know God better. Ministry matters only when it causes behavioral changes in someone's life. This is in harmony with the object of God's love and God's redemptive power. That is the outcome of ministry.

Essential to this ministry outcome is an understanding of the human organism. Ministers who do not have a grasp of human nature are crippled in any attempt to administer God's grace. However, one does not have to acquire an understanding of the human experience from reading books or attending classes. Long before there was ever anything called psychology, there were men and women of great wisdom and intuitive skills who were very effective ministers. Throughout the history of the church, there have been those who have never had a psychology class, never read a psychology book, or never really thought analytically about psychology. But they understood themselves and others, and God blessed their efforts. Many individuals who have no formal training in human behavior have a wonderful touch with people.

While acknowledging that some people have intuitive skills in dealing with others, why not take advantage of a study of human behavior? If there is some systematic way of analyzing the human experience, should not that be explored? Consider the case of any missionary. If one accepts a call by God to go to a people who speak a foreign language, the Holy Spirit will anoint him for that ministry. On the other hand, if God calls an individual to go to a foreign country, and if it is possible before going to learn their language, their history, their habits, and their culture, it would be a terrible neglect to fail to take advantage of that God-given opportunity.

It is very much like preaching. If a minister is called upon to speak the Word of God to a group of sinners, but has had no time to prepare, the Scripture says he could just open his mouth and the Lord would fill it (see Luke 12:11,12). Under those circumstances, he can speak with clarity, intelligence, and persuasion. However, just because such a promise of divine intervention is given, it would be foolish for a minister to consistently walk into the pulpit, depending on that promise as a substitute for preparation.

It is prudent to take advantage of all the available possibilities of training, knowledge, analysis, and learning, in order to refine ministry skills and improve effectiveness. Only then can one bring all human efforts humbly before God and honestly say, "God, take this modest set of skills, this very small bit of information, anoint it by the Holy Spirit and make it an effective vehicle for communicating the Word." In doing so, God blesses all aspects of any effort for Him. The Holy Spirit still takes over and becomes a divine enabler. The minister works and prepares for ministry activity—a sermon, a counseling session, or worship service—as if everything depended on him, and he prays as if everything depended on God.

A most important aspect of ministry preparation is understanding the human experience. To reach such an understanding, the minister needs to take advantage of what psychology has discovered about human behavior. At the same time, psychology should not be overestimated. It does not have the ultimate answers; it cannot change one human heart; it cannot remove the stain of sin. But within its limits, psychology has enormous value to ministry. It is a tool for opening one's understanding of people, so the minister, through the work of the Holy Spirit, can bring the grace of God to their needs.

Psychology and the Scientific Method

While psychology is rather young, as far as human ideas go, human behavior has been studied for centuries. Only about 125 years ago did people begin to use the word *psychology* or begin to think of human behavior as something that could be analyzed. Human behavior had been studied in a fairly informal, casual way, one person at a time. When anything is studied in this fashion, superstition gets involved, wrong conclusions are deeply ingrained, and folklore emerges.

Psychology began, not when human experience started to be studied, but when it started to be studied systematically. It is the study of human behavior that is done in a scientific way. How does psychology differ from sociology and anthropology, since they are also scientific studies of human behavior? Sociology studies human behavior in groups; anthropology studies the human behavior of large cultures; and psychology studies the human behavior of a single behaving organism. That is really the only difference. There are few clear lines of demarcation between them. In fact, it is hard to know when psychology ends and sociology begins. For example, if one is being studied individually, that is psychology. If one's marriage is being studied, that might be regarded as sociology.

Human behavior is difficult to study scientifically, as opposed to geology which is the study of rocks. A rock can be brought into a laboratory or set on a post. The scientist can shine a light on it, weigh it, bounce sound waves off of it, photograph it, poke it, chip at it, or do whatever he desires. The objective methods of science, in cold, calculating, laboratory approaches can easily be applied to the study of rocks. Physiology, the study of the way the body works, is somewhat more difficult, but it can be studied scientifically, normally using animals. A rat can be brought into a laboratory and put on a pedestal just like the rock. The scientist can shine a bright light on it, poke it, photograph it, and do all kinds of things to it. The rat will not be quite as cooperative as the rock, however, because it has feelings, it is going to squeal and try to get off the pedestal. It is going to be a little harder to expose to the rigors and the routine of science, but the objective methods of science can be accomplished with a rat.

A scientist cannot bring a human being into a laboratory, put him up on a stool, shine a bright light on him, and chip away at him. He cannot do the things to a human being that he can do to a rock or a rat. If he wants to study, analyze, and understand humankind with the same degree of precision and clarity that he can study the rat or the rock, he has to develop more complex systems to do that. Thus, psychology, the scientific study of humans, is much more difficult than physiology or geology.

If an individual wants to be a psychologist and a Christian, he can be. If he wants to use his psychology to understand what makes people go to sleep in church, that is doable. If he wants to use his psychology to understand why some people leave home and go far away to college and some want to stay within 25 miles, he can. If he wants to use his psychological analysis to determine how long his sermons ought to be or even to determine what kind of clothing one should wear to a job interview, he can do it. But when he goes beyond the things that can be analyzed by science, into the affairs of the heart and the spirit, God throws up a stop sign and says psychology cannot go there. These things can be known only by the Spirit of God. That is a very important distinction.

> Let me illustrate out of my own experience: I have studied psychology at three good universities: Georgia State University, Emory University, and Harvard University. At those places, they never told me that the soul of man was beyond the means of science, because many do not see man as God's creature. The typical, secular, nontheistic psychologist, sees man as a creature that just somehow evolved and pulled himself out of the goo and finally evolved into a human being. They have missed the image of God in man, and they believe psychology can fully explain this organism. I, along with thousands of other Christian psychologists and hundreds of thousands of men and women of faith who have effectively used the work of psychology to do their jobs in their ministries better, started at a different place. I started with the fact that we are God's creatures, that His image is in us and it is stamped on us in every way. I am not a rat. I am not a rock. I am made in the image of God, and I can use the methods of science to understand behavior up to a point. And at that point, I can go no further.

Viewing man as God's creature is the approach this course will take to look at the methods of science. The results of psychological research will be used to better understand oneself and others and thereby enhance one's opportunity to have a more meaningful ministry.

2 PERSONALITY

By Robert W. Fisher, Ph.D.

Personality is a topic that psychologists have been attempting to define and study for a long time because personality is what makes each person a unique individual. So, personality theorists (psychologists who study personality using a scientific methodology) have been trying to understand what personality is. Every individual has a personality. But what makes some shy and others bold? What makes some leaders and others followers? That is the idea behind trying to understand personality. When one looks for a way to define personality, each theory presents a different explanation of how it develops. To summarize what personality is, for the purpose of this study, the following statement is a useful definition: "Personality is deeply ingrained patterns of behavior that evolve from a combination of innate and learned tendencies which are modified by life experiences."

First, this definition contains the idea of "deeply ingrained patterns of behavior," suggesting that personality is not a single act or passing conduct. In this definition, *personality* is said to contain "persistent, consistent, and deeply ingrained patterns of behavior." And where do they come from? They come from a combination of innate or inborn characteristics and learned tendencies. The patterns of behavior that form personality, essentially who one is, come from a combination of both innate or inborn temperaments, and life experiences or learned tendencies. One's experiences shape and mold him within the framework of his inborn predispositions. The second part of the definition speaks about "learned tendencies which are modified by life experiences." This is important, because even though personality is consistent, it is not fixed, meaning that it can be modified. As learning occurs, the individual is changed in some way through the learning process. Personality, then, is fairly consistent and permanent, and it is derived from a combination of innate or inherited characteristics and life events—learning experiences—that mold and shape the individual throughout his lifetime.

Nature Versus Nurture

The complex interweaving of these tendencies and these experiences is one of the big issues that psychologists who study personality have dealt with for many years—the issue of nature versus nurture. Nature is the "impact of heredity," and nurture, is the "impact of experience." Consequently, the question is always there: Which plays the greater role? Is an individual more the product of heredity (nature) or more the product of experience (learning)? This is an issue about which there is little agreement.

What is agreed on, however, is that every human being is a unique individual, and that some combination of heredity and life experience, both of which are totally unique to an individual, makes the person the way he or she is. Each person has a unique genetic heritage; each person has unique life experiences. Thus, when studying people, one looks at a different specimen in every person—that is the essential meaning of the word individual. When one studies chemistry, element A and element B can be measured precisely and combined to produce AB in each experiment. Chemists can replicate or repeat an experiment, because when the same chemical elements are combined in the same way, identical results occur. There are no identical results in human behavioral research: people are the products of their own unique genetics and their own unique set of experiences; therefore, they can never be viewed the same.

Individuals constantly change through daily experiences. This does not mean that there should be no attempts to study human behavior. It does mean, however, that the task is more difficult and the results of the study are less precise. Furthermore, these results should be viewed with caution until vast amounts of research produce vast amounts of data that consistently point to similar findings. One way to distinguish how nature and nurture make people the way they are, is to use analogies. One analogy is to think of nature as providing the basic sketch of one's personality, and one's life experiences filling in the details. Another analogy is that inheritance, or nature, provides the skeleton of personality, and life experiences, or nurture, are the things that add flesh to the bones.

Another way of looking at personality differences is to think of the impact of nature, or inheritance, as being like the grain in wood—it runs all the way through. The wood plank can be painted with several layers of paint, but when those paint layers are stripped away, the same wood grain reappears. Similarly, the inherited, or innate, aspects of personality seem to keep reappearing. There are certain temperamental dispositions, certain aspects of who one is, that are inborn and never seem to fully change. They can be covered over. They can be modified. They can be shaped in certain ways, but certain tendencies always seem to be there, underneath the surface behavior.

Interesting animal research has been done in this area. Animals have been shown to have different characteristics and tendencies. Some are shy animals; some are curious animals; some are frightened animals—animals with predisposed tendencies to certain temperaments. Researchers have attempted to teach shy monkeys, those that are less aggressive, to be more exploratory and more outgoing, with some pretty good results. By putting the monkeys in a secure environment, they were able to teach these monkeys to be risk takers—to be somewhat more willing to go out and explore their environments. Researchers found, however, that when those same monkeys were put in situations of stress or fatigue, they tended to fall back to their old natural personality style. Their learned characteristics tended to fall away, and they tended to revert back to the more natural state. Personality, even in monkeys, is a complex interweaving of tendencies. A basic sketch is provided by nature and then that is fleshed out by adding detail through life experiences.

Personality Theories

Theorists who have studied personality through the years can place their studies into four categories. These are psychoanalytic theory, dispositional or trait theories, environmental theories, and representational theories.

PSYCHOANALYTIC THEORY

The first category is psychoanalytic theory—the field that was pioneered by Sigmund Freud in Vienna, Austria, in the early 20th century. One could say that the scientific study of human behavior began with the anecdotal notes of Freud's observations of his patients, and personality theory began with Freud's human development assumptions. Individuals who follow some form of this approach, practice psychoanalysis and are psychiatrists. They have a degree in medicine with a psychiatric residency. Freud was the father of psychoanalytic theory and furnished much of the language of analytical thought, even though his theories have been significantly modified since the late 1930s. Freud believed that personality is driven or motivated by internal forces and that who one is and what one's personality is come from forces within. He thought that some tendencies were innate and some were learned.[1] Psychoanalytic theorists believe that early

---

[1]Editor's Note: Freud posited that every individual was a closed system, a single universe. He believed that the child was born with all the energy that it would ever have, and the way that child or adult developed depended on the way that his energy (which he called libido—sexual energy—for Freud all energy was the same) was directed and used. Freud's expression for the utilization of energy was "to cathect." Any single use of energy was a "cathexis."

life experiences shape and mold personality. Since childhood is viewed as predisposing adult personality and behavior, great importance has been placed on early childhood development.

DISPOSITIONAL OR TRAIT THEORIES

The second category of theories is the dispositional or trait theories. These theorists believe that personality is made up of certain characteristics, or traits. All people possess these traits to a certain degree, but in different amounts. For example, in a trait like emotionality, the tendency is to be very emotional. One who is less emotional would be described as having that trait or disposition to a lesser degree. Sociability, artistic tendencies, even something like being optimistic, a leader, or a risk taker, are all characteristics or traits that would define a personality. So, the idea of trait theory is to try to understand personality based on certain traits or characteristics that all possess, but in different amounts.

ENVIRONMENTAL THEORIES

A third category of personality theories is the environmental theories. These theories emphasize nurture—how one is shaped by external learning experiences. External situations exert pressure on the individual, molding and shaping him into what he becomes. To the environmental and learning theorist, something within does not determine behavior; life experiences and formal learning shape the individual's behavior patterns. Some environmental theories use terms like *behavior pattern* to replace a vague term like *personality*. B.F. Skinner, the noted Harvard experimental psychologist, held this view. In fact, his animal research led him to conclude that each person is the result of circumstances and life experiences or history of reinforcements. Change has to come from the outside in, rather than from the inside out.

REPRESENTATIONAL THEORIES

The fourth category of personality theories is called representational theories. This view suggests that personality is a reflection of the ways that an individual perceives and represents himself and the world around him. With this view, actual behavior (objective reality) is not as important as the way in which behavior is perceived (perception is reality). What really makes the difference in behavior is how it is perceived: how one perceives himself, how he perceives other people, and how they respond to him, based on their perceptions. For example, someone might be, by most objective standards, physically attractive. If, however, that person perceives himself as being ugly, he may never be convinced that he is attractive, because his perception is that he is ugly, despite the objective reality. If people are perceived as being hostile or trying to take advantage of others, whether they are or not, others will likely respond to them as if they were in fact hostile. This view is represented by Carl Rogers and Abraham Maslow. They believed that in order to institute change, one must help people change the way they perceive themselves and have a more realistic perception of the way people are actually treating them. Representational theory, then, suggests that personality is based on how one perceives himself and the world around him.

This short overview gives a brief look into the role of personality theorists and some concept of the way psychologists have attempted to understand and explain what personality is, what it is made up of, and how it impacts people. In the final analysis, personality is probably some of all that has been written and a combination of all the theories that are presented.

Other Personality Issues

There are important issues that personality theorists confront in trying to understand why people are the way they are and what makes up personality. One of those issues is the idea of *free will versus determinism.* Free will versus determinism is the argument of whether behavior is controlled by the individual or determined by outside forces. Some psychologists believe that the person has no self-control or free will; everything one does is programmed or shaped by the environment. Conversely, other psychologists believe that individuals do have self-control and free will. However, most psychologists probably fall somewhere in the middle. While the environment places certain constraints on the individual and certain boundaries around him, within those boundaries one can choose how to act and how to behave.

Victor Frankl wrote an excellent book on this topic called *Man's Search For Meaning.* Frankl, a Viennese psychiatrist, spent three years as a prisoner in World War II concentration camps. From that experience, he was able to glean an interesting perspective on human nature. The first half of the book recounts his experiences in the concentration camp, and the second part of the book talks about the view of human nature that he developed from those experiences. He said he had a unique opportunity to see human nature stripped down to its barest existence. As prisoners, everything was stripped from them. They had nothing left but their very lives. One gets an interesting perspective on human nature when life is stripped of all material possessions down to just mere existence.

Frankl saw the effect on the people in the concentration camps as they all found themselves in the same circumstances: prisoners, held against their wills, all rights taken away, and being held under the constant threat of death. Frankl concluded that the environment did not determine their behavior, because if that were true, they should all act the same way. But they did not. He noted that within the constraints placed upon them, some behaved like saints. Some of the prisoners took care of their fellow prisoners by sharing what little food they had. Basically, they did whatever they could to be helpful to those around them. Other prisoners in the exact same situation behaved like swine, taking food from weaker prisoners, and betraying fellow prisoners to the guards. They behaved abominably. Frankl concluded that the environment did not dictate this heinous behavior. Within the constraints of the horrible circumstances of a concentration camp, some chose to behave in a very kind way, while others chose to behave in a very selfish way. It was a choice of the people themselves. So, free will versus determinism, is the argument of whether one has free will over his own behavior or whether it is determined by the environment. The behaviorist would say those who acted like swine had a history of reinforcements that would not let them act any other way. In the middle, between Frankl and Skinner, is where most psychologists are more comfortable. In other words, most believe that the environment creates certain constraints and boundaries for the individual, but within those boundaries he chooses how he is going to behave.

Which Is More Important: Childhood or Adulthood?

Another issue that psychologists have dealt with in the study of personality is, Which is more important: childhood experiences or later life experiences? Some psychologists, like Freud, believed that early childhood experiences set the tone for personality and very little change takes place afterward. To Freud, almost all that is important in development occurs before age six; in fact, the basic personality is formed by age 5. Other psychologists feel that childhood is not that important. They feel that later life experiences are really more important. Carl Jung, who was a student and a colleague of Freud's, felt quite the opposite of Freud. He felt that childhood was really just a period of growth physically, emotionally, and cognitively, but that the really important things that went into the shaping of the individual's personality did not come until later in life. Jung taught that only in the later years of adulthood does one become the individual he was really meant to be.

Which, then, is more important: one's early childhood experiences or those later life experiences? Research has shown that early childhood experiences do tend to set the tone for personality. In fact, they set the tone for life. But that does not mean the individual cannot change, or continue to grow, adjust, or modify behavior. Since early life experiences are crucial for setting the tone, most psychologists who are child experts emphasize the importance of helping children get a good start early in life. If they have a solid foundation early, they can withstand much of the storm and stress which come later in life, especially in adolescence. Any children who have good role models and who receive love and a sense of security early in life have a better chance for developing strong, healthy personalities.

Motivation: Biological or Psychological?

Another issue in psychology is the role of biological motivators versus psychological motivators. Is man basically subject to his biological urges, or is he motivated primarily by higher psychological and spiritual motives? Living in a finite body, each person is subjected to its physical weaknesses, as well as its strong urges. Life is a constant struggle to control the body's appetites and live a balanced life. But to suggest that only bodily appetites motivate people, severely limits what human beings are. Most psychologists believe that people are more than just biological urges; they do have psychological aspirations and goals; they have a spiritual dimension which motivates them; and they have higher mental functions. Research has shown that aspirations and goals can elicit transcendent responses from the individual.

Basically Good or Basically Evil?

Personality theorists have discussed yet another issue: Are people basically good or are they basically evil? Scriptures settle the issue for believers. Human beings come from Adam's race with a curse, in need of a Savior. Only by being born again can the fallen nature be cured. Many psychologists, however, feel that human beings are basically good, and if they are allowed to grow and develop without hindrance, they could become happy, successful people. This seems to suggest that when people are denied certain needs or certain emotional satisfactions, they cannot develop in a positive way. Anecdotal observations of the behavioral history of men and women are heavily in favor of the biblical view. This view is an optimistic one; because in God, basic human nature can be changed, and there comes to each person a hope found only in a spiritual life. That hope is a new beginning, a new birth, available to every person.

Conclusion

So, what can be taken from this lesson? The fact that the people with whom one comes into contact, whatever the relationship, are individuals who need to be understood. They can be better understood if one looks at them from the following three perspectives: uniqueness, complexity, and inconsistency.

First, each person is unique. People are the product of their own unique heredity and their own unique set of life experiences. There is no way to place individuals into a mold. There are no absolutes when it comes to understanding personality. Each person is different. The goal is to understand each person as an individual based on unique life experiences, and in understanding each one, come to treat each person as a unique individual to be treasured for what he or she is and can become.

Second, people are highly complex—the most complex creatures on the earth. Innate forces, biological urges, social expectations, psychological forces, all combine to make people into the types of individuals they are. To understand people, means to understand that they are made from different dimensions and different influences.

Third, people are inconsistent. The only consistent thing about human beings is their inconsistency. Human beings are subject to mood swings and the feelings of the moment. Everyone has experienced what it is like to feel good one day only to have the bottom fall out the next day. One might seem to have the patience of Job one day, and a short fuse the next day. What accounts for this? While some of it is biologically determined, a lot of it has to do with just the way human beings are—inconsistent in their approaches to how they understand the world, how they perceive the world, and how they perceive themselves. If people remember that each human being is unique, that each is highly complex, and each is, to some extent, inconsistent from day to day, and even from hour to hour, they can begin to better understand each person and themselves. That is one of the most important lessons that can be learned from the study of personality.

3 DEVELOPMENTAL PSYCHOLOGY

By Jerome Hammond, Ph.D.

The discipline concerned with human development from conception to death is called developmental psychology. This complex branch of psychology deals with the developing human organism in three ways: cognitively, physically, and emotionally—or mind, body and spirit. The developmental views expressed in the course will be, primarily, those of Erik Erikson.[1] Erikson extended Freud's stages of early childhood development to include the whole life of the individual. Erikson also replaced the somewhat weird and widely unacceptable Freudian concepts of childhood sexuality with a view of human development that was based on social interaction.

---

[1]Editor's Note: Erikson presented his views to a 1948 White House Conference on Children and Youth, and subsequently published his stages of human development in a monograph entitled *Identity and the Life Cycle.*

Early Interest in Child Development

Before looking at Erikson's stages of development, it would be helpful to understand how knowledge about the developing human organism began to unfold. In the 19th century, Philip Aires did research in human development. His interest was the development of children. For hundreds of years, observations of development had dealt only with childhood, because most of one's development was perceived to have been completed during childhood. Aires studied art to see how children were perceived, and he conclude that children were generally viewed as young adults because they were so often pictured as dressed in adult clothes. In fact, children were not regarded as they are today, but thought of as being adultlike and should, therefore, be treated as adults.

Consequently, children were not as likely to be cuddled and cherished as children are today. Instead, they were thought to need training and discipline and were often treated harshly. One of the reasons for this harsh treatment was the misuse of the doctrine of original sin. With the church's dominance, combined with the doctrine of original sin, the parent was taught that their primary function was to remove evil from the child with discipline. When children acted out, disobeyed, or were selfish, original sin might be blamed, requiring the parent to punish the child severely. It was not uncommon to withhold food and water from the child in order to humble the child, in order to break that child's will, and to save his soul. In extreme cases, there was even legislation that allowed the parent to take the child's life, if the parent deemed it necessary in order to save that child's soul. For centuries, children had very difficult lives.

Rousseau's Revolt

In the 17th century, a theory emerged, holding that children were not born with original sin. Children, Jean Jacques Rousseau insisted, were like a flower-innately good. The reason, Rousseau contended, that children acted badly was because society was essentially evil and influenced the children to become evil. Left alone, like flowers, children would unfold into beautiful individuals. Rousseau believed that the key to having a society free of evil, crime, and bad behavior was to allow children to grow naturally. The doctrine of original sin that dominated the Middle Ages and dictated how children were treated was confronted by the Rousseau philosophy of innate goodness and his demands for society to let children grow naturally and free of adult domination.

John Locke and Tabula Rasa

In reaction to the biblical teaching of the doctrine of original sin and Rousseau's theory of innate goodness, came the theory of tabula rasa. Espoused by John Locke, tabula rasa, meaning "blank page," held that children were neither innately evil nor innately good. Locke's theory taught that children come into the world as a blank page with nothing written on it. Locke said the role of adults, of society, and of parents is to write something on that blank page.

The doctrine of original sin, as practiced by the church in the Middle Ages, and the philosophy of Rouseau were basically reactive. On the other hand, John Locke's tabula rasa was proactive, insisting that society and parents can make a difference in the life of the child. In its most extreme form,

Locke's views taught that society could make of that child's life whatever it desired, because society had an opportunity to write on a blank slate-the tabula rasa. Parents were now seen as responsible for what the child came to be. Society placed demands on parents who were now in a panic to know how to create a novelist, a scientist, a doctor, or a philosopher.

The result was an enormous demand for research into child development. Questions such as these were investigated: What will bring about the optimal level of development in children? How much discipline is needed for the child's development? How little discipline? How much reading? How early? How much can the child learn? At what age do children learn? What kind of knowledge can children master? Likewise, the impetus arose for research into the best way to rear children.

Thus, with John Locke's theory, research in developmental psychology began. Today, it is understood that there is no tabula rasa. It has been discovered that children have certain predispositions. It is known that children are "prewired" when they are born, and have the ability to begin processing an enormous amount of information soon after they come into this world. Developmental psychologists have shown that from birth, children begin growing, learning, and being influenced. Likewise, research has shown that one can guide children in a certain direction, but inevitably children tend to go the direction to which they are predisposed.

In its early days, research in developmental psychology tended to center on peak performance—how the individual grew faster, stronger, and gained more knowledge. Later, research also centered on loss of function—how one declines, losing physical strength, mental facility, and memory function, eventually moving toward the cessation of life.

Nature Versus Nurture

One of the great debates in psychology continues to be the nature versus nurture question. There are enormous amounts of research on both sides as psychology continues to grapple with the question of which is the greater influence—heredity or environment? The catch phrase, nature versus nurture, continues to generate interest in the public and the psychologist. While research into how people learn once seemed to favor environmental factors as determinants of development, the vast knowledge emerging in the field of genetics may have tilted the argument in the direction of heredity. The question will remain open for some time as research continues.

Contextualism and Human Experience

Another concept of what influences humans is called contextualism. Contextualism is made up of three components: *age-graded experience, history-graded experience*, and *nonnormative experience.* A normative age-graded experience is something experienced by everyone who is a part of one's age group. As people move through life, they tend to have similar experiences at the same point in their lives. They are cohorts. People who go through adolescence have normal age-related experiences. For example, people fall in love for the first time at about the same age or men begin to shave at about the same age. These are normative age-graded experiences that influence their development.

The adolescent's perspective of life may be very optimistic, and he may think that the world offers him great opportunity. However, the person who is going through midlife transition may understand that life is brief, because more than half of his life is behind him. These two groups are going to have different perspectives on life; in fact, these perspectives result from normative age-graded influences.

There are also normative *history-graded influences.* For example, one generation will vividly recall that Ronald Reagan came to power during their formative years. Another generation will remember that John F. Kennedy became president during their formative years. One who grew up during the Reagan or Clinton eras will have a different perspective on life than one who grew up during the Eisenhower or Kennedy eras. Our parents or grandparents who grew up during the Great Depression of the 1930s will have a very different perspective on saving money than one who grew up during prosperous times. Thus, personal experience of history significantly influences development.

Nonnormative experience is an event that is not typical of one's lifestyle. It is typical that everybody will go through elementary school and have certain experiences. It is typical that individuals will go through adolescence and have experiences peculiar to adolescence. Those are normal experiences. A nonnormative influence is an atypical experience, whether good or bad. Not many people win the lottery, but it is life altering. In addition to having to deal with numerous relatives who suddenly show up, one has to deal with changes in lifestyle, new tax brackets, and, perhaps the media. Other nonnormative experiences might be a natural disaster, or an airplane crash. These are life changing and they are context-related experiences that shape development.

Reality and Perception

Perception is another fundamental principle in understanding behavior and development. One's perception of reality and the attending behavior to that perception become relevant to development. If one perceives that another intends to harm him, his reaction will reflect that perception whether the perceived behavior is true or not. What controls behavior is the perception of intention. In interchange with a person at any age, one must seek to understand that person's perception of reality, not what is truly reality. If people perceive that they have heard God's voice, they are going to behave in a particular way. Has God spoken to them? The answer to that question may not be as important as what they perceive and really believe. If one's perception is that a spouse is unfaithful, then he or she is going to react accordingly. What is the reality? While the answer to that question is very important in the long-term, it is irrelevant in understanding the individual's immediate reactions and relevant behavior toward the spouse. Where does that perception come from? Perception comes from those predispositions and experiences that have been discussed: from heredity and environment, from age-graded influences, from history-graded influences, and from unique or nonnormative influences.

Erik Erikson and Development

In developmental psychology, Erik Erikson is a stage theorist. That is, Erikson finds that all people go through stages in life. This occurs with continuity and discontinuity of development. *Continuity of development* suggests that individuals develop from one stage to another in a smooth series of changes with no discernable difference between one stage and the other. One does not go to bed one evening unable to talk and wake the next morning able to talk. Continuity of development implies a gradual developmental pace like a child developing the ability to walk. First, the child lifts its head and then moves the arms and legs. Then the child begins to crawl. Next, he pulls up and stumbles around, hanging onto furniture. Eventually, the child lets go and takes the first step. That is continuity of development.

Discontinuity of development suggests there are leaps in development—very rapid changes, followed by a plateau, and then another rapid increase in development. This is exemplified in language development. In early childhood, a toddler may learn a dozen words in one day. In the period of 24 to 30 months, language ability may jump from a few words to several hundred words. Erikson suggested that humans are a blend of continuous and discontinuous development.

Erikson studied under Freud's daughter, Anna Freud, a significant psychologist in her own right. Sigmund Freud advocated a theory of development based on stimulation of erogenous zones, a part of the body that gives pleasure, during the early years of life. Freud taught that an erogenous zone needed proper stimulation for proper development. Too much or too little stimulation of an erogenous zone caused developmental problems. Personality development depended on appropriate stimulation in an erogenous zone at the right time. This is a gross oversimplification of Freud's stage theory, but the point is not to understand Freud. The point is to understand how Erikson's views changed the Freudian theory of childhood sexuality.

FREUD REVISED

Erikson taught that development was not psychosexual but psychosocial. Erikson meant that humans develop through social interaction with other people. These people help the individual to define who he is. If he believes that he is witty or humorous, Erikson said that is a result of other people letting him know that he is funny. This perception crafts an identity of being humorous. The same may be true of intelligence or of inferior feelings. If one feels inferior to other people, where did that come from? Erikson would say inferior feelings are the result of social interaction in which the people with whom one interacts have sent a very strong message of inferiority.

A second way that Erikson revised Freudian theory was in the extension of the developmental stages. Freud ended his developmental theory at adolescence, believing that most development ended at adolescence. Somewhat pessimistic, Freud believed that while it might be possible that a person could come through the childhood developmental stages perfectly and get just the right amount of stimulation in the erogenous zones at the right time, nobody does. Therefore, everyone needed psychoanalysis. Freud believed that since development essentially stopped at adolescence, people needed psychoanalysis to correct what had gone wrong during childhood. In contrast, Erikson taught that development does not stop at adolescence. He was convinced that development goes on throughout adulthood and continues even to the end of life. By using the word "development," Erikson did not mean that one only gets better. Erikson essentially meant by development that one changes—with performance increasing in childhood and decreasing in old age. He understood that change goes on throughout life.

Perhaps Freud and earlier developmentalists thought that development only went through adolescence because that is the time when development is most easily observable. They may have postulated that development stopped after adolescence, because in a short period of time, enormous physical, emotional, social, and linguistic changes occurred which were readily observable. While one is not able to see much change during adulthood, Erikson showed that there is also an enormous amount of change throughout life. In children, observable changes occur and development is primarily external. In adults, unobservable changes occur, and development is primarily internal.

OUTWARD TO INWARD DEVELOPMENT

When a child begins to interact with the world, that interaction is physical. Everything they grasp goes to their mouth. Lacking the capacity to deal with the world intellectually, interaction with the environment is physical. Place a child in a room with strangers, and the child will be uncomfortable and hold onto their parent. Eventually, the child will wander away from the parent, continuing to look back and reference the parent. That is a physical action. Looking back, mother or dad is still there, and the child feels safe to continue to explore this new environment. Children are terrorized if they are left in a room and suddenly the parent disappears for a moment.

As the child gets older, the child will continue to reference the parent, and the family, but development will go inward. The child will no longer look back physically, but he will continue to look back mentally. That could be one of the reasons that divorce is so devastating to children. Psychologically, the child can no longer look at the parents for the stability and safety that was present when the parents were together. Divorce might be tantamount to the child looking back as an infant and the parent being gone. When parents divorce, it is like the child being left alone, and it is a terrifying experience for many children.

Development always moves from the outside to the inside. Before language acquisition, a child will pick up objects and hit another child when he wants something or when he is frustrated. As children get older and become socialized, they are trained not to hit other children. As they develop intellectual capabilities, specifically language, hitting becomes internal and a child will hit with their words, using names to injure. Development is moving from the external to the internal.

In midlife and especially in late adulthood, development parallels childhood, even though development has moved internally. People still have fears. They still have needs. They still have concerns and desires, but those needs have now moved inside. It takes more ingenuity and more care to search out pressing developmental issues and adult needs at the end of life.

4 ERIKSON'S PSYCHOSOCIAL DEVELOPMENT STAGES: PART ONE

By Jerome Hammond, Ph.D.

Erikson believed that a person develops psychosocially. By this, he meant that social interaction is a primary determinant in human development and that the circle of social interaction becomes larger with age. There is one important person in the life of the infant—the primary care giver, usually the mother or father. This primary care giver, whoever it is, feeds, nurtures, and provides almost all of the social interaction the infant experiences. With increasing age, the child's circle of social interaction expands to siblings, extended family, playmates, members of the community, schoolmates, and friends. As the circle of interaction gets larger, development is influenced by the people involved in interaction with the individual.

Erikson's Eight Stages of Development

Erik Erikson proposed eight stages of life through which all individuals pass. Everyone does not stay in these stages for the same amount of time, but each one goes through all eight stages in the same order, and once a particular stage is reached, one never regresses or goes back to an earlier stage. For Erikson, each stage presents a particular developmental crisis. That crisis is the major task or issue to be faced and mastered at that stage in life. The outcome can be good or bad. The outcome of one's handling of the crisis of a particular stage will determine the results of that period of development. The residue left over from the way one handles the major crisis in each developmental stage will carry over to the next stage and affect one's ability to successfully master the crisis in the next stage of development.

Crises bring changes in development. If all one's needs were constantly met, that would constitute a womb environment and the person might never seek to change. Development flows from frustration. When a prelingual baby is hungry, the infant learns to cry. In the womb, the child had no need to cry, because all of its needs were met. It was comfortable, warm, and constantly nourished. Outside of the womb, the child has to learn to call on its mother for milk. The child has to learn not only if it wants the bottle, but if it wants what is in the bottle. Does it want milk? Does it want juice? Does it want cola? If he is handed milk when he prefers juice, out of frustration he learns to indicate juice instead of milk. Erikson assumed that to encounter crises or frustration is to foster development.

TRUST VERSUS MISTRUST

Erikson called the first stage of development *basic trust versus mistrust.* This is the major issue for the first year of life. The crisis revolves around this question: Does the primary care giver create an atmosphere that engenders trust or fosters mistrust? Erikson says this first year of life will lay the foundation for one to become a trusting individual or a suspicious, mistrusting individual.

How does this happen? The womb provides an environment in which all needs are met, but now the infant, rather violently, enters a new world. This new world is, by comparison, very hostile. Tension in this environment is primarily physical. The child is very hungry, and there is no way to get that need met unless a care giver regularly and faithfully feeds the infant and fulfills this basic need.

Since the infant enters this first year of life not knowing how to communicate, trust rests completely with the parent. Totally helpless, the newly born infant is completely dependent on the ones who give life-sustaining food and care. When one is in a situation where help is desperately needed, a sense of trust builds. Conversely, when the help is not there, a sense of mistrust develops.

Programs in which corporations send their executives, powerful CEOs and CFOs, out to the woods in camouflage outfits to climb ropes across the water and swing in trees is an attempt to teach basic trust. They may be required to create a survival plan that builds a sense of teamwork to learn trust in one another. An executive may be placed on a platform to fall backwards into the arms of people who are waiting to catch him. The idea is to build a sense of trust. The person is in danger of serious injury if those other people do not catch him. The idea is to make oneself vulnerable and to put oneself at risk in order to build trust in those who have vowed to care for him. This is the same idea Erikson was trying to communicate in his first stage of development: basic trust versus mistrust.

Since the human organism is completely helpless at birth, a child's cries are as though it is crying out in a sense of life or death. It is as though the child thinks: *If I cannot communicate to these people that I need nourishment, I will die.* This primary care giver is keeping it alive. Out of that relationship comes this tremendous sense of gratitude. The child will become aware that, although completely helpless, he or she has survived because of this person. If an executive, falling backwards off a platform while his peers catch him, finds a real sense of trust, imagine how powerful this bond of trust is between the infant and the person who cares for him when he is completely helpless.

If, in this atmosphere, the child feels all his needs are being met—when hungry, he is fed, when cold, he is warmed, when upset, he is comforted—Erikson says there develops a deep sense of trust. How strong is that sense of trust? Erikson said that it is equal to the sense of helplessness that child feels. Because that child feels absolutely helpless, he or she also feels absolute trust. From that bond of trust, the foundation is laid for an unbreakable parental attachment.

Erikson says that if parents do not create this atmosphere in which the child feels comfortable and safe, and feels like their needs have been met, then it develops a sense of mistrust. The child is suspicious of a world that cannot be trusted. Eventually, the child develops the idea, *This is a place where I am in danger, where I will not necessarily be cared for, and at all times I have to watch out for myself.*

Erikson suggested that a balance is needed. A person who is completely trusting, to the point of being naive, is in one kind of danger. A person who is totally suspicious and can never trust anyone becomes dysfunctional in another way. One should understand that there is bad and good in the world, but there are people who can be trusted.

In this first stage, Erikson explains that the child does not understand the concept of self. He does not understand that there is a difference between himself and the person who is giving him care. He does not perceive *I am myself and that is my mother* or *I am myself and that is my father.* The child makes no distinction between these two entities. In his mind, all is one. The child is totally egocentric. In other words, there is nothing else other than himself. He is the entire universe. When the mother or father meets the child's needs, the child believes that they are meeting their own needs. So, when the child cries and someone brings a bottle and puts the bottle in the child's mouth and the child is full and satisfied, the child does not perceive, *here come my parents and they are feeding me.* In the early months of stage one, Erikson says, the child thinks everything is a part of himself. So, when he cries and is fed, he believes he is feeding himself. The significance of that theory is that if the child's needs are met, the child begins to trust himself. These are the roots of the development of a strong ego. The child trusts his parent, learns to trust his world, and learns to trust himself all in this first year. All of this depends on meeting the child's needs.

Most child psychologists, therefore, believe that a child cannot be overcompensated in the first nine months of life. That is, the child cannot be held too much, or comforted too much. If the child is crying in the first nine months, the child has a need that is not met. It is not because the child is trying to be manipulative. If the child is not hungry, or wet, or in pain, the child has a psychological need. The child needs to be comforted. This view holds that no child can be spoiled in these first months of life. The child cannot be held too much or rocked too much. After nine months, one may choose to let the child linger in the crib, but not from birth to nine months.

AUTONOMY VERSUS DOUBT AND SHAME

Erikson called the second stage of development, *autonomy versus doubt and shame*. In the first year, the child has had his needs met and learned to trust the parent. Now, as motor skills develop, the child can get up and walk around or walk toward an object. This is the time to develop a sense of independence. Erikson believed that the human organ- ism is always attempting to achieve these two things—independence and identity. Children become somewhat independent as soon as they can crawl, but as soon as they can walk, they are running away from mom and dad to explore their world. Excited about learning, when they can run to another room or run to a brightly colored object, they will. Naturally protective, the parents' normal reaction is to forbid. The child runs toward an object, and the parent attempts to stop the child's experimentation. With no idea how their world works, a child knocks a glass off the table and the glass shatters into a hundred pieces, and the child has done something glorious in his own mind. He knocked this object off the table and for some inexplicable reason it fell to the floor, shattered, and made this wonderful noise. The child thinks, *This is great. Let's do it some more.* This child is experimenting, exploring. This is why the age is called the terrible twos.

Parents are eager, of course, to prevent children from breaking the china; therefore, they must forbid this behavior. Unfortunately, the child hears the word "no" so often that "no" becomes his conversational baseline. It does not matter what one asks the child; the answer is "no." "Do you want to go outside? No. Do you want to stay inside? No. Do you want to get up? No. Do you want to get down? No." The primary reason that child uses the word "no" so much is that it is a word that he has heard. Whatever he touches, he hears the word. He wants the car keys. "No." He wants something off the table. "No." He wants to go outside. "No." A very forbidding world is created, while at the same time the child has the ability to move about. He can explore, and there is an excitement in exploring his world. For the first time, however, he experiences denial. Even though he desperately wants to go over and play with these things and even though he has the capability, he is not allowed to.

Erikson suggests that if parents are not creative, they will impose an atmosphere of shame and doubt. In a sense, the parent is God to that child. Why? Look at how physically imposing the parent is. Imagine being two feet tall, and everyone else stands six feet tall. Essentially, that is what it is like for a child interacting in an adult world. Not only are the parents huge, but they also make all the rules, and enforce all the rules. When they are forbidding to that child, it is tantamount to the

Lord himself forbidding them to do something. The child naturally wants to explore, but if the parent is constantly saying "no, stop, do not do that, do not go there," a sense of shame and doubt can emerge in the mind of the child.

This shame and doubt comes from children believing that this world is too complex and that they cannot figure it out. They know that every time they reach for something, every time they go somewhere, they are told not to do that, and thus conclude that it is best for them to just stay in their place and not try to explore this world. The children who are very curious, can come to doubt themselves, and become ashamed to try when there is punishment at every turn. Erikson says that parents should create a safe atmosphere that allows children to explore. Do not become too forbidding, but keep the child safe and allow him to explore.

This atmosphere helps create a curiosity in the child. A strong curiosity maintains a sense of initiative when the child knows that he can function and understand how the world works. When this results, a sense of autonomy and independence evolves. First, parents gave the child a sense of trust in the first stage of development because the child believed that someone was going to take care of him. Out of that a sense of autonomy emerges. Now, the child can explore the world and be safe, and the parents have provided an environment where initiative will thrive in the next stage.

Toilet training and autonomy. A big issue in the stage of autonomy versus doubt and shame is potty training. For the first time, the child must internalize discipline. For the first time, the child is told, "When your body tells you to do something, ignore that impulse and control your body." To change the child's diaper is a favorable action, but at some arbitrary point, the parent wants the child to be potty trained. At that point, the parent has to teach the child to wait until he has a designated place to go to the restroom. Imagine how difficult this is for a two- or three-year-old. All his life, he went potty anytime and anywhere he pleased. Suddenly, this authority figure, this "god" in his life, says to him, "Not yet, you have to wait." The child is asked to exercise control. Then he is asked to internalize this discipline—not to wait for mom and dad to discipline him, but to discipline himself.

If the parent puts too much pressure on him while potty training, Erikson says the child gets the message that he is not strong enough to control his body. He thinks, *My body is in control, not me.* At first, and for some time, he cannot control his urges. His reaction is, *It's too difficult. I can't do what my parent is asking me to do. My body is stronger than my will.* If, on the other hand, the parent goes slowly and works with the child, over a period of time, the child learns to control bodily functions and learns that he is stronger than his body.

Erikson says that out of this issue of potty training—the understanding of who is in control, the will or the body—a lesson is translated for the rest of one's life. In all habits—physical, eating, studying—where there is a battle between the physical world and the intellectual world, the winner comes out of the resolution of the crisis of potty training. What is the difference between the athlete who can jog 25 miles and the athlete who can jog only 10 miles? Erikson would say potty training was a primary factor in the one being able to say, *Even though every cell in my body is screaming stop, I am stronger than my body. I don't care if my body wants to stop, I'll keep going.*

At the French Open Tennis Tournament in Paris, Michael Chang was having severe leg cramps, to the point of being unable to stand. The match was delayed for a therapist to work on his legs. He would gut it out for a couple more games and collapse again with leg cramps. Ivan Lendl, seeing his condition, worked hard to complete the match, but with great fortitude, Michael Chang fought through all of the pain and physical agony to win the match. It was a most exhilarating tennis match and display of courage. What made it so incredible was Michael Chang's ability to say, *I don't care how badly my body wants to stop, my will is stronger than my body.* Erikson would say that ability for the will to dominate the body could come from this potty-training issue.

INITIATIVE VERSUS GUILT

Erikson's third stage of development is initiative versus guilt. The child has come through autonomy versus doubt and shame. He has learned about the world, begun to explore and learned many of the social rules. In this stage, Erikson says the child is going to test the limits of the rules. He begins to interact with kids out in the neighborhood, and experiment with the rules. The crisis is leadership.

During the stage of initiative versus guilt, a group of kids are playing kick ball by the normal rules. At some point during the game, one child will suggest, "You know what I think? Everybody should get three kicks instead of one." This child is taking the initiative. The child is saying, *I know what the rule is. Let's try a slight twist to the rule. So, I'm going to take a very dangerous initiative, I'm going to try to change the rule.* To this point, all the rules are set. Children rarely question the rules, until this stage of initiative versus guilt. At this age, the child will take a very big risk to try to change the rule and see what happens. There are two distinct possibilities. The children can reject the idea of three kicks and toss this kid out of the game. Or, the kid with the new initiative can win them over and create a consensus for three kicks for everybody. A leader emerges, Erikson says, and suddenly this kid learns how to get other people to follow. The kid becomes a risk-taker and believes other people will follow. In this third stage, initiative versus guilt, the child begins to interact with a larger social circle, taking chances, and according to Erikson, out of this stage leaders emerge.

5 ERIKSON'S PSYCHOSOCIAL DEVELOPMENT STAGES: PART TWO

By Jerome Hammond, Ph.D.

In discussing Erikson's first three stages of human development, it was noted that almost all the social life of the child is in the home with the family. A small amount of social contact may occur outside the home, but the social interaction of the child in Erikson's first three stages is with parents, siblings, and primary care givers. The five-year-old child is about to make the first significant social change in its young life.

INDUSTRY VERSUS INFERIORITY

Erikson's fourth developmental stage is *industry versus inferiority*. The focus is on the early school years—five or six years of age through preadolescence. Social interaction moves outside the home to the school. For the first time, the child experiences a significant influence from individuals other than parents or primary care givers.

In the home environment, social interaction has come from people who love the child, who think he is great, and who have told him constantly how treasured he is. Every social interaction has reflected a homogeneous perspective on life. As the child moves into the stage of industry versus inferiority, social interaction begins with people—teachers and children—who are very different, and have worldviews and lifestyles the child has never known.

The social and psychological impact on the child in the wake of his new life, however, is a much more important consideration. Social changes are exacerbated and made even more severe as the important issue of self-esteem begins to unfold in the wake of industry versus inferiority crises. The major crisis confronted during this period is developing the confidence to feel that one can perform great feats and accomplish important things based on a growing sense of self-worth. The outcome of the crisis of this period will be determined to a large extent by whether the individual acquires high self-esteem or low self-esteem. The resolution of that crisis will predispose one to an achievement orientation, or to a timidity that flows from a lack of confidence and a feeling that one is incapable of achieving at a high level.

Erikson reasoned that since most social interaction to this point in life comes from family, and since parents have a tendency to exaggerate the child's good qualities and ignore bad qualities, the child may have an unrealistic view of life. Parents, of course, normally have positive evaluations of their children. Their perceptions of their child, though honest, may not be accurate, however, when measured in the cold reality of open competition. A parent may believe that his son is a potential all-state quarterback and communicate that to his son. But the day may come when the son faces a more talented child and has to compete with that boy for the right to be the first-string quarterback. To tell a child that he or she is absolutely the best—the best ball athlete, the best at math, the smartest, or the most beautiful—may seem to be a way to build self-esteem, but there is a potential downside. Parents' tendencies to use these superlatives when referring to their son or daughter, may inflate the child's expectations out of the realm of the reasonable. Erikson said that psychosocial development is a result of the people with whom one interacts. Since this child has known only the family and has been told throughout life that he or she is the most intelligent person in the world, there is a high probability that the child will believe this and define himself or herself in that manner.

All at once, the child enters the stage of industry versus inferiority, and abruptly moves into the social interaction of the school. After having heard how smart he is and how well he can read for his age, the child concludes that he is a terrific reader. It is not uncommon for a parent to exult with words like, "You read better than anybody I have ever seen for your age." In the first month of school, he will compare himself with all the others in the class. Now he begins to see realistically, for the first time, whether he is the best reader in the world. Of course, he now knows he is not the best reader in the world. It could be that he is not the best reader in the class, and he may even be the poorest reader in the class. This is of less importance educationally than it is from a psychosocial perspective. The reading deficit can be cured if the child's deflated expectations do not give him a lifelong sense of inferiority.

When self-esteem is attached to a level of performance, that is, when one thinks that he is great because he is the best reader in the world, then one's psychological foundation—so vital to the development of a healthy personality—may be seriously damaged when reality is seen. If self-esteem is attached to performance, and performance is significantly below expectation, then the child's self-esteem may be so seriously affected that feelings of inferiority begin to undermine this child's personality development.

What then is the answer? The parents were trying only to encourage the child by building confidence when they told him he was the best reader in the world for his age. This is understandable, and while it is important to build self-confidence, that cannot be accomplished by basing showers of affection on exaggeration and myth. It is unwise to attach self-esteem to performance. It is also a mistake to attach self-esteem to qualities that can change when the child compares himself to other children—and the child will make comparisons.

If the child has been given an unrealistic view of his or her ability, self-esteem will suffer when the child faces reality. On the other hand, when self-esteem is attached to characteristics like honesty, generosity, helpfulness, or trying one's best, those qualities are not affected when comparing one's own performance to another person. Honesty is something that is not variable when compared to another person. If the parent says to the child, "You are a wonderful person because you are so generous," that is not going to change when compared to a peer. That value remains constant.

Industry versus inferiority comes from what Erikson describes as the child's need to do something well. At the age of four or five, the child is very happy just to participate. They merely want to be in the game. This is obvious when observing a group of kindergarten children at play, dressed in their little soccer shorts and shin guards, running back and forth in a sort of comical chorus line. They run en mass to one end. The goalie kicks the ball, and as a group, they run to the other end. The other goalie kicks the ball, and the group runs merrily back to the other end of the field. This is what they do for five or six games. The season is over, and everybody gets a picture, a plaque, and a party at Pizza Hut. They feel great because they participated.

Once the child gets deeper into the stage of industry versus inferiority, everything changes. As the child nears adolescence, he not only wants to be on the team, but he also wants to play a significant part. It is no longer enough for the child just to get a uniform, a plaque, a picture, and a pizza party. That child wants to get into the game, score a goal, and become one of the contributors to the team. In today's sport's vernacular, he wants to be a "go-to-guy." This sense of, "I can make a contribution" is what Erikson called industry. At this age, children want to feel that they can really make a serious contribution to the team, the school, the family, the Sunday school class, or to whatever they are a part of. This is the feeling the parent should cultivate in the child.

In a competitive environment, self-esteem based on comparing oneself with another, cannot be prevented. This is not a bad trait unless the comparisons have been exaggerated out of proportion to reality by well-meaning, but unrealistic pronouncements of biased parents. If self-esteem is not attached to performance in acompetitive climate, children will make their own comparisons and tell you who is superior at one thing and who is better at something else. Then, they can take joy in participating even if they are not the starting quarterback or the smartest in the class. They have not disappointed either themselves or their parents. This admonition is not against high expectations or the pursuit of excellence. The warning is against creating unrealistic expectations in a highly competitive climate where a child, pumped up by exaggerated parental perceptions, is pushed into competition they cannot possibly win.

Since children develop the ability to do abstract work, as well as stronger bones and muscles at different ages, a separation in ability occurs near adolescence. Some children are better athletes; some are better readers; some are better at ballet; and another is best when playing a particular instrument. For example, a father indicated that his son was shy and isolated until the day a trumpet was placed in his hand. His life was changed. Immediately, he excelled in performance with the instrument and soon in other areas of his life. Today, he is a successful college professor and is the principal trumpet player in a well-known symphony orchestra. However, children may lose the joy of participating when they see they are not as skillful as others in some area. They may express a desire to drop out. The key for parents and authority figures is to help the child discover where he is talented and point him in that direction. Let him see something that he does well, even though someone else may be a little better. Emphasize that one does not have to be the best, but he has need to give his best. If he does, sooner or latter, he will reach his personal best. That could be a family record or it might be a world record. The tendency to emphasize that only number one is good creates a "number one syndrome." Everybody wants "to be like Mike," but in all of history, there has been only one Michael Jordan. It is, therefore, very important in the industry versus inferiority stage to (1) emphasize something the child does well (2) encourage him to strive for excellence (3) point out that he does not have to be number one to be successful, but (4) show him how important it is to give his personal best effort.

In this stage, children are a joy—cooperative and eager to help. However, it can be frustrating for parents during this time, because children's skills are slower as they learn to do things that are easy for adults. Most of the time it is much faster for parents to do it themselves, but the child needs and wants serious interaction and a sense that parents value their help.

Family research has shown that studying farm families provides useful data. In the Midwest area of North America where farm families still work the land, incidents of juvenile delinquency and divorce are significantly lower. Family researchers believe that this happens because Midwestern farm families have cohesion. They hold together over generations and encourage the development of a sense of industry. Children understand from a very early stage that they are an integral part of the work of the farm, and they learn to be industrious. They can see that if they do not carry their share, someone else will have to do what they failed to do, or this farm will not survive. They are not patronized; they have a real job and contribute something important to the farm and the family. Such an environment gives the child an authentic sense of importance, of accomplishment, and a bond to the family. This is precisely what Erikson was emphasizing. Children need to feel that they make a real contribution. "I am not just a member of this family; I help it survive." Responsible parents allow the child to become a vital part of family life.

For example, when Mother is working in the kitchen, it would be much faster if the small child would move out of the kitchen and let her clear the dishes, the mother reasons, *Then we will do something interesting.* That is exactly what the child does not want. The child wants to make a contribution in the kitchen—to go to the dishwasher, get the plate out, hand the plate to her mother, and let her put the plate up. It is slow and tedious, but it is critical to developing a sense of industry. Another example is Dad working in the yard. It would be easier to trim the hedges and then do something together. But the child wants to work in the yard with Dad. Building a sense of industry and a work ethic, develops in settings like these. The sense of joy that flows from a job well done, comes from learning the lessons related to the crises of industry versus inferiority.

IDENTITY VERSUS IDENTITY CONFUSION

In adolescence, the primary issue is *identity*. Erikson later amended his stage theory saying that while the search for identity begins in adolescence, the search for identity continues for the rest of one's life. As the circle of social interaction enlarges, one encounters different views. At some point in adolescence, one has encountered enough views to ask, "What really is my view? How do I feel about certain issues in my life?" A certain amount of crisis in life is necessary to force an evaluation of, "What do I believe? Where do I stand? Who am I?" In adolescence, the decision is being made by the person—not according to church, gender, culture, school, context, or family, but according to the individual himself.

Erikson says the identity search leads one to consider ideas that were heretofore assumed. Virtually everything in life is analyzed. The dominant society says, "Act this way." The church says, "Act this way." Growing up, if parents said the children should be a particular way, they accepted it. They wanted to meet the expectations of their families, cultures, gender, and schools. Their views of how they should act and what they should be were accepted without question.

Sometime during adolescence, however, one starts to see that there may be contradictions between the way the church says one should be and the way one's culture says he should be. There may be a contradiction between what parents say one should be and what the church says one should be. There is often a conflict between what the dominant society thinks is right or wrong and what the parents teach. The identity crisis involves a searching of all these influences and choosing what one wants to become. Sooner or later one may have to say to his parents, "I'm not that way, Mom and Dad. I love you, but I believe this way." Or one may have to say to a friend, "That's not the way I believe; I can't go along with you." Erikson says it is critical that the person make these vital evaluative decisions in developing his personal sense of identity.

Society sees many sides of a young person during this period. Young people are constantly experimenting with clothes, looks, hair, and behaving in a different way every week. What is going on? The adolescent is exploring—discovering who he is. Perhaps he is asking himself: *Does the way I look please me? Do I really want all these holes in my jeans? Am I a person who likes an earring? Am I a person who likes my hair to stand straight up? Do I want to work on white water rafting for the rest of my life, or would I rather become an accountant and earn some good money?* The problem is that they do not know. So, Erikson says one needs this window of time, which is basically adolescence, as a frame of reference for exploration. This is a time to test the limits—ask questions about faith, parents, school, culture, gender, and everything in life. They should emerge from this time of adolescence with an identity, a sense of who they are. They could emerge with an identity confusion, lacking a clear sense of identity. Emerging adults, with an inadequate view of self or sense of identity, tend to allow other people to define who they are. Although parents find it difficult to encourage young people to explore those issues and reach a sense of identity, if they do not, identity confusion may result.

INTIMACY VERSUS ISOLATION

The next stage is *intimacy versus isolation*. Erikson says one cannot be intimate unless he or she has established an adequate sense of identity. As one begins to forge an identity and discover who he is, the way is paved to discover other people. During this time, the young adult will either develop long-term, intimate friendships or begin to live in isolation. The development of long-term intimacy in relationships becomes a foundation for the important social structure—marriage and family—that dominates one's life throughout adulthood. If these relationships are not formed, periods of isolation dominate the life that should be experiencing intimacy. While intimacy versus isolation follows identity versus identity confusion, they are actually closely woven together.

GENERATIVITY VERSUS STAGNATION

After intimacy versus isolation, and young adulthood, the next stage is middle adulthood—*generativity versus stagnation.* This is the period of midlife transition. Erikson says that to the middle adult, one's experiences may have resembled something of a lifetime conveyer belt, moving him through life. Culture has dictated much of the individual's life, telling him where to go to school, who to marry, what careers to choose, and what projects to undertake. In this stage, Erikson suggests that a powerful psychological shift occurs. It happens to people in varying degrees of intensity. There is a gender difference, but everyone—men and women alike—experience a midlife transition. The focus shifts from "How long have I lived, to how long do I have to live?" The result is that people begin to reexamine their lives. They begin to think more about what is important to them. If they have gotten on this conveyor belt of life, so to speak, without much thought or identity formation, then it leads them to get off and refocus. Sadly, many people decide that all they have done is of such little importance that sometimes they abandon family and friends to begin another life.

This reaction to the midlife crisis results from a failure to adequately resolve the search for identity in adolescence. A sense of despair accompanies the realization that one is nearing the end. There is less time left than has expired. When one's accomplishments do not measure up to expectations, the sense of crisis that began back in one's youth leads to a discontent with life and an immature reaction to these continuing identity pressures. If, on the other hand, one knows that this is who he is no matter what others expect, and has been able to form close, long-term relationships, the crisis of generativity versus stagnation will be resolved in an understanding that "This is who I am, and I did what I felt like I should do in life. I can leave it all to the oncoming generation with the realization that I gave something. I don't have to throw it all away and change it all. What I have done is good."

In order to invest in the following generation, there arises another aspect in the ability to maintain long-term, intimate relationships. This aspect of intimacy is the ability to pour oneself into someone who follows—to have a close relationship, to confide, to trust, and to mentor. The individual who is unable to pour a portion of his life and time into the next generation, will retreat into isolation, disengage from society, and stagnate.

INTEGRITY VERSUS DESPAIR

Erikson calls the final stage of life a time of *integrity versus despair*. This is the time where it is obvious that the end is near. That does not mean the last week of life, but a time in life when the last chapter is being written. What was done in youth and middle age is complete and cannot be changed. Whether there was accomplishment or failure, it is too late to go back and repair the past. Earlier in life, a certain window for recovery existed—a time to recover from mistakes—but those days are gone. In the stage of integrity versus despair, one loses that sense that "I can fix it." Erikson says people look back over their lives and ask themselves, *Have I done it the right way? Have I lived my life to the fullest? Have I done what I thought was right? Have I invested my time wisely? Do I feel a sense of integrity?* These questions are made even more poignant by the realization that life will soon be over and nothing can change that fact.

If one looks back at life with a sense of wasted time and squandered opportunity, life in the final stage will be difficult. When one feels that the family has been neglected, the children were not the object of much investment, time has been wasted or spent building something that is meaningless, he has a sense of despair: *I had one life and I really wasted it doing things that are unimportant to me now.*

This is the reason why many people suffer depression in late adulthood. Erikson observed that men, in particular, may have a difficult time in this stage.

In this culture, Erikson observed, women tend to invest their lives in the children. Men tend to invest their lives more in things—in getting a home, in climbing the corporate ladder, and so forth. More often, men get to the end of their lives and regret that they did not invest more time in the lives of the people they really loved. When people understand that this stage is coming, they desperately want to have lived life the right way, not only in the things that they have built, but also in the way that they have interacted with people.

It gives one a sense of integrity when he or she can look back over the years and think: *I made mistakes, but I'm pleased with my life. I loved God. I expressed love to my family. I worked hard. I kept faith with my values. There it is. With what I was given, I did the best I could, and I would enjoy living the same life again.* With this sense of integrity, there comes a peace with one's life in the final years.

6 DEATH AND DYING

By Jerome Hammond, Ph.D.

In Erikson's stage of integrity versus despair, the person in late adulthood is depicted as preparing for the end of life by looking over the past and assessing the kind of life he has experienced. If one feels good about his life, then he has a sense of integrity. If not, he feels a sense of loss, of wasted opportunity, and an intense sense of despair. With a sense of either integrity or despair, there is a keen sense that life is coming to an end. This leads to the final issue of human development—the issue of death and dying.

This topic is one which most people find uncomfortable. In fact, death and dying seem far removed for those of the younger generations. The issues of death and dying are not often addressed unless one is in a profession that deals with these issues. For example, the ministry is often called upon to assist families who face crises relating to death and dying.

Not only is the subject of death an ignore topic in this culture, but also the elderly are often hidden from view. They are not featured in the mass media like young people are in this culture; therefore, the elderly are relegated to obscurity. There are areas of the country where people in late adulthood live in huge communities of 50,000 or more. Even cemeteries have been removed from churches, and people are not reminded of their fate when they attend church services. Aging and dying have been removed from people's thoughts until the last moment. Nevertheless, death should be seen as an event for which one prepares in this life.

Hospitals and Hospices

There are two different institutions where people are sent when they are dying—hospitals and hospices. A distinct difference exists between the philosophy of a hospital and the philosophy of a hospice. To a hospital, death represents the cessation of life and is the enemy. The hospital's goal is to do everything possible to prevent death. This can be a hostile and unsympathetic environment for the terminal patient. This is not a criticism of a hospital, but an observation of the hospital's purpose. The medical community has been effective in preventing death, and for that they are held in high esteem. Sometimes, however, that philosophy is not the best, particularly when death is imminent.

The philosophy of the hospice, in contrast to the hospital, is that to continue the struggle against the demise of the organism may not be in the best interest of the terminal patient. The purpose of a hospice is to keep the person comfortable until death comes. Those who work in a hospice understand the philosophy that death is a part of life, that death happens to everyone, and that their role is to help the patient through this period until death comes. A hospice generally is a warm place where the people are more sympathetic toward pain and the relief of pain. A hospice feels more like a personal residence with warm colors and the amenities of home. These two institutions treat people who are dying, but with different ideas about how to approach death.

Children and Death

It is important to examine how death is viewed in this society through the different developmental stages. What do children think about death? Children cannot understand or even conceive of what death is before the age of 5. Children do, however, experience separation anxiety. This phenomenon can be observed in young children when they see their parents leave a room or when they are left at day care. Children experience separation anxiety because they lack object permanence and also because they have become aware that they are a different entity from their parents.

Object permanence is the child's ability to understand that just because something is out of sight does not mean that it does not exist. Show the child a small rubber ball and they become interested in it. Cover the ball with a cloth, and the child will become disinterested in the ball and look around for something else to do. When the object is out of sight, for them, it ceases to exist. As the child becomes older, he achieves object permanence. Then he can understand that when Mom and Dad walk out of the room, they are not gone forever, but still exist. When children gain object permanence, they also understand that there is a difference between themselves and their parents, but they also suffer separation anxiety. When the parent leaves, the child understands that the parent still exists, but he wants him to come back, because he knows he is separated from his parent.

In the experience of a death in the family, children only understand separation. When a young child loses a parent, he thinks the parent has gone away for a long period of time. He does not understand that the parent is gone permanently and will not fully conceive of that until 8 to 10 years of age. To tell a child that his mother is in heaven and hear him repeat this, does not mean he grasps a complex concept like death. Children first understand that the parent is gone and will not return, then they gradually begin to grasp the concept of death. This occurs between 5 and 10 years of age. When children reach the age of 9 or 10, they begin to understand that everyone dies, including themselves. Parents should discuss death and dying with children when they are curious, in age-appropriate terms that will not frighten them.

Adolescents and Dying

Adolescents think about death and dying in a very different way than children or adults. Adolescents experience a phenomenon called personal fable. Personal fable is a form of egocentrism, holding the concept that one is very unique. This serves as a shield around adolescents that seems impenetrable and blocks them from thinking about injury, death, or circumstances that could bring pain and suffering into their lives. Adolescents believe they are unique. They express this to their parents in a time of frustration, particularly when it comes to romance, with a comment such as, "I know I am in love. You don't know what love really is." What makes adolescents believe that they are the only ones who know what love is all about? That comes from this sense of personal fable, of being unique. To adolescents, their thinking, feelings, and experiences are all unique. They think that the love they feel is so deep, no one has ever felt this kind of love before. In Shakespeare's *Romeo and Juliet*, the two lovers are examples of adolescents with this sense of personal fable. Romeo and Juliet thought their love to be so great that life was not worth living without the other.

Surrounded by this impenetrable shield of personal fable, adolescents believe that they are somewhat immortal. Other people get sick, get injured, and die, but it will not happen to them. Adolescents will frequently warn their friends to be careful and not engage in high-risk behavior, then engage in that same risky behavior they warned friends against. They will drive recklessly without a seatbelt, because they feel that tragedy only happens to other people; it does not happen to them. Therefore, adolescents do not think about death very much. They may joke about death and even put themselves in situations where they challenge death, but to them, death and dying are very far away. Even when there is a death of a close relative, a parent, a sibling, or a friend, the adolescent continues to live in denial. Death does not apply to them.

Adults and Death

Throughout young adulthood (20s and 30s), a person usually does not think about his death. Even if they experience the death of parents and grandparents, young adults are too busy with their own families and careers to conceive of themselves as dying. To them, death is a distant concept. They understand what death is about, but it is not something they want to deal with until they get to middle adulthood.

Individuals from 40 to 60 years of age fear and worry about death more than any other age group. The powerful psychological shift of going from how long they have lived to how long they have to live, leads them to think about their own demise. While in later adulthood, people think more about death and dying, the important distinction is that people in middle adulthood worry more about death and dying. In late adulthood, there is an acceptance that this is the end of life and one needs to make preparation for it. In later adulthood, friends, siblings, and parents have gone, and dying is a real part of one's personal experience. Death is not something in the future to be feared, but something that is going to happen and should be accepted.

Facing One's Own Death and the Death of Others

Two more important areas to examine in looking at this topic are facing one's own death and dealing with the death of a friend or loved one. Dr. Elizabeth Kubler-Ross has suggested five stages of death and dying. These observations, like all psychological research, apply to everyone generally, but no one specifically. Therefore, not all individuals experience all these stages in the order suggested by Dr. Kubler-Ross. However, these are the stages one may experience when confronting one's own death.

DENIAL AND ISOLATION

The first stage is denial and isolation. After a diagnosis that one has a short time to live, there is a refusal to accept this fact. A typical response is that the doctors do not know what they are talking about. Cases may be cited where other people have had a similar diagnosis and it was wrong. Other opinions may be sought, and these too may be denied if they also give the prognosis of imminent death. The dying individual may isolate himself from others who are seeking to help him in facing his eventual death. If the parent is dying, the children need closure, but the parent may refuse to talk about it. Denial and isolation when facing death can be dysfunctional for the family until one accepts the fact that, apart from divine intervention in the form of a miracle, he is going to die. Since the shock that one is dying is overwhelming, it can render that individual unable to function. Therefore, one's denial may be useful for a brief period, but gradually, he must accept the fact of eventual death. If, however, one persists in denial and refuses to interact with anyone about his death, he will isolate himself and contribute to a dysfunctional environment.

ANGER

According to Dr. Kubler-Ross, once a person understands his prognosis, he will often have the attitude that he can conquer this illness. While that is a healthy attitude, it can become dysfunctional if taken to the extreme. However, once a person understands that he cannot beat this sickness, then he moves into the second stage—anger. He may be angry at the physician for giving this diagnosis or for not finding this sickness earlier. He may accuse the physician of incompetence and talk of lawsuits. While accepting the fact of personal terminal illness, he needs someone to blame. He may even express anger toward God. These powerful emotions can continue to isolate friends and family.

BARGAINING

The third stage is bargaining—an attempt to change the outcome. The person may try to bargain with God by promising the Lord that he will serve Him and live a better life: "I'll do whatever you want me to do, Lord. Just please give me a little more time." Another way a person may bargain is to seek out alternative forms of medicine and healing. Abandoning traditional Western medicine, one may try Eastern medicines, herbs, and different techniques in an attempt to change his fate. Ultimately, the person is going to see that these attempts will not change his destiny. Death is coming no matter what he does.

DEPRESSION

When that transition takes place, the person will begin to experience the fourth stage—depression. At this time, the person pulls back from acquaintances and from social interactions of any kind. He wants to be alone. The person disengages from life psychologically. He is preparing himself to leave this world. He may sit alone in a room and look at photo albums, remembering life experiences, often with tears.

ACCEPTANCE

Finally, the person reaches the last stage—acceptance. At this point, one will usually reengage with loved ones and friends. During a period of closure, realizing that the end is near, one will say things that he has always wanted to express. These will be very sensitive and meaningful times for the individual and his family.

According to Dr. Kubler-Ross, not everyone goes through every stage, and not everyone goes through every stage in the same order. One's faith and spiritual orientation may avert all five stages. In other words, one may go from diagnosis to acceptance. On the other hand, one who has lived the most religious life, may go through every stage. Thus, the role of one who is befriending the dying individual is simply to let him go through the stages naturally. Do not try to force him through in a faster manner. Do not try to sway him from his feelings. Simply be there for him as he goes through these difficult times.

The Death of a Loved One and the Grieving Process

An important area to discuss is how one copes with the death of a loved one. There are three stages: shock, painful longing, and resumption of normal life.

Shock

The first stage of loss is shock. In the first month following the death of a loved one, it is common for a person to be extremely emotional. The experience of shock may be manifested by crying at inappropriate times. Sitting at the dinner table with friends, the person who feels this incredible loss may begin to weep uncontrollably in the middle of dinner. These emotional episodes usually last about a month. The person is trying to adjust to the emptiness he feels. The responsibility of the care giver is to let him go through this stage without trying to move him through it quickly, or trying to stop him from crying, or trying to assure him that everything is going to be okay. One should allow the grieving person to get past this time of shock and adjust to the fact that the loved one is gone. Crying, even in the middle of the day, is a common and healthy way to move through this stage of the grieving process.

PAINFUL LONGING

The second stage is painful longing, recalling memories of the lost loved one. This period manifests a focus, almost an obsession, to remember the loved one and talk about him. He will recall how they met, their life together, and what a great friendship they had, and he may look endlessly through photo albums. This stage may last from six months to two years. The care giver should let him go through this sense of pining and longing even when the grief of this stage causes bouts of insomnia and mild depression.

RESUMPTION OF NORMAL LIFE

The final stage is resumption of a normal life. Having moved through the grieving process and flushed out all of these emotions, an ordinary life with normal social interactions resumes. The individual has moved past his obsession with the loved one who died, and is back into a typical social life. This usually happens in about a year after the death of a loved one, but can take up to three years. If the grieving of the second stage goes beyond three years, one should be advised to seek professional help to move past the grieving period.

7 ABNORMALITY

By Robert Fisher, Ph.D.

In a discussion of abnormal behavior or abnormal psychology, the logical place to start is to define what is meant by *abnormal.* Most people who are asked what abnormal means, say that it means "not normal." That circular definition does not shed any light on the question.

What Is Normal?

To understand what is meant by *not normal,* one has to begin with an explanation of what *normal* is. This is difficult because there are few absolute norms for human behavior. Is any behavior normal behavior in all cultures? What is viewed as normal in the American culture often changes in another culture or context. Being depressed and crying is not viewed as behaving normally; however, if one has lost a loved one, this is normal behavior, at least for a period of grieving. If someone covers his face with orange and white paint and engages in yelling and screaming, he would not be exhibiting normal behavior, unless he were attending a University of

Tennessee football game. In that setting, absurd behavior seems the norm. So, normal behavior has to be judged in the context in which it is occurring, that is, the circumstances surrounding it and the culture in which the behavior exists. Before psychologists defined *abnormality* as "a deviation from what is normal or optimal," abnormality was defined by set ways of behaving. However, this approach to defining abnormal is not effective, since it is so difficult to determine what optimal behavior is. That would introduce a value judgment, saying one behavior is good and another is bad.[1]

Deviation and Normal

An example of the problem of defining behavior as deviation from the optimal would be identifying the appropriate way a person should respond in a stressful situation. Should one respond calmly and without anxiety? That depends on the way one needs to respond. For example, individuals may respond differently to an important examination—one may be calm and another anxiety ridden. Thus, normal is what works to the best interest of the individual who is performing in a stressful environment. This situation presents the difficulty of defining optimal or determining the best way to act in stressful predicaments. When the value judgment about which way is best is introduced, the definition of normal

[1]Editor's note: This discussion is not about morality or moral values. Obviously, some behavior is morally good and other behavior morally bad. The author's reference to good and bad behavior in this context is a discussion of the problem of identifying personality attributes that determine whether responses are normal or abnormal (i.e. good or bad).

loses objectivity. That is why most psychologists now define abnormality statistically, or a deviation from the norm, rather than a deviation from the optimal.

Abnormality, then, is "a deviation from the average." That becomes a more useful statistical definition. Deviation from the average means that one's behavior is different from the majority, but not necessarily good or bad. That is the rationale for defining *normal* statistically.

The value judgment is removed, and behavior is viewed in terms of the behavior of the majority of the population. This means that everyone is abnormal in some way. If one drives a Ford Taurus, he is not normal, since most people do not drive a Ford Taurus. If one wears Hush Puppies, he is abnormal, because the majority of the population does not wear Hush Puppies. That does not mean one is good or bad based on that deviation from the norm. It just means that one is doing something that most people do not do.

Nonconformity Can Be a Problem

In some instances, being a nonconformist is more effective; however, an extreme instance of nonconformity may become a problem behavior. There are three ways to determine whether behavior is a problem. First, if it causes an individual ongoing distress and suffering, then it is a problem. While short-term distress often results from the loss of a loved one or from a severe disappointment, when it becomes chronic, it is a problem. Second, if behavior interferes with one's ability to function by causing problems in maintaining relationships, it is a problem. This difficulty can interfere with job performance and ability to function effectively. Third, behavior is considered a problem if it causes harm to oneself or to others. The presence of anyone of these factors suggests the behavior needs to be addressed.

Mental Disorders

In abnormal psychology, these types of problem behaviors are often the result of a mental disorder. The word *disorder* suggests that the behavior is not orderly—it is confused, out of order, and not normal. Mental disorder is the term used to define problem behaviors that cause people stress, to be unable to function effectively, and possibly to lead them to harm themselves and others.

These types of disorders usually have a complex combination of influences. For example, a mental disorder often has a *biological origin*, sometimes a *sociological basis*, or it may be *psychological in nature*. Mental disorders may have a biological basis that combine disordered behaviors with nonproductive thought patterns. One might say that most mental disorders are a volatile mix—a little biology, a little psychology, and a little social behavior—combining to create the problem. In assessing the dilemma, psychologists and psychiatrists will look at many factors: medical conditions, abusive environment, social relationships, role models, relationship problems, career challenges or work problems, and financial pressures. Mental disorder may result from a confluence of all these factors. In particular, childhood experiences might have predisposed an individual to this behavior. Over and over, early childhood abuse is implicated in the development of mental disorders. Childhood abuse seems to create fertile soil in which disorders will grow. Consistently, psychological research shows that an individual who develops mental illness, not chemically induced, had a disturbed childhood environment.

Depression

To understand how biology and behavior combine to produce problem behavior, the mental illness of depression is a good example. Depression is sometimes referred to as the "common cold" of mental illness because of its frequent occurrence. It is estimated that 15 percent to 20 percent of the population has experienced a form of depression. This was expressed in such forms as sadness, feelings of emptiness, despair, a lack of interest in life, a negative view of oneself, or withdrawal from normal activity. When one observes these symptoms, the person is probably dealing with a type of early-on depression. Research has shown that it is not just a psychological issue, but biological and social factors also contribute to it as well. Certain chemicals in the brain regulate mood, and if those chemicals are disrupted or imbalanced, they can cause an individual not to be able to reach the elevated mood level needed to function effectively. This is not using biology as an excuse or blaming biology alone. With a depressed mood level, negative thought patterns are also present. The person is pessimistic about life—he thinks poorly of himself; he has feelings of helplessness and hopelessness; his minimal effort produces poor performance. This behavior, so characteristic of depressed individuals, is usually the result of biological, psychological, and sociological factors, combined with nonproductive negative thinking.

Treatment of Mental Disorders

Treatment of a mental disorder, such as depression, must include all three dimensions—biological, sociological, and psychological. Treating someone who is depressed may indicate a need for medication—an antidepressant drug—which helps to restore the balance of the chemicals in the brain that regulate mood. But drugs alone are not enough. Along with the medication, one needs psychological intervention to help break faulty thinking. Self-blame, feelings of helplessness, and a sense of hopelessness form a cycle of negative thinking that needs to be broken.

When one is depressed, he withdraws from relationships and normal activities. Then, he needs to be taught to rebuild social skills and get back into life again. Recovering from depression involves more than prescribing medication. Medication can restore physiological balance, but a pill will not restructure faulty thought patterns or social skills. This requires psychological and spiritual intervention.

The Minister's Role

Many problem behaviors, like early stages of depression or anxiety, can be helped by a sensitive, caring and compassionate minister. Most ministers will not encounter many seriously ill people, but they do need basic knowledge and information about mental disorders and how to refer those who appear to have serious mental problems. So, it is important for ministers to experience some form of counseling and counselor training. Perhaps, the most important lesson for the minister is to be able to recognize when a person shows signs of problems that are beyond his ability and training.

The next step is to learn where and how to refer the person to a psychiatrist, a clinical psychologist, or a counseling psychologist who is trained to deal with serious mental illness.[2]

How should a minister personally respond to people with these issues? One should follow the model of Christ. In studying the way Christ related, one sees a sincere love for people. He was open and honest in His communication with them. He was empathic, compassionate and sensitive to their needs. He had a nonsmothering concern for people and understood what they were feeling. He built relationships with people whom society had treated as outcasts.

Human behavior is the result of a complex combination of forces, and when one interacts with others, he becomes part of their social milieu. It is as if one becomes a thread in the fabric of their lives. Thus, it becomes one's Christian duty to make sure that the thread he becomes in that fabric is a positive thread. When someone has an encounter with a believer, he should be better for the experience.

[2]Editor's Note: Until recently, mental health professionals sometimes blamed religion and faith for contributing to mental illness. Now, in every major metropolitan area, there are psychiatrists and psychologists who, as people of faith, treat mental disorders without attacking the patient's faith and view faith as a contributor to good mental health. It is important for the minister to identify these kinds of professionals in making referrals.

In fact, a believer should have a constant prayer that the Lord will help him to have a positive impact on the lives of the people with whom he interacts. God forbid that they should feel worse after having an encounter with a believer. The prayer of all believers should be: "Lord, help me to be one who lifts people's spirits, rather than one who pulls them down."

One other factor is very important in working with people—the ability to listen. One's attending behavior cannot be emphasized enough in training for ministry. This is true, because when a person seeks the help of a minister, he is usually out of options. Emotionally drained, people reach out to their ministers, needing more than anything else, the warmth which they can provide. Listening to people and being totally compassionate, gives them the immediate dignity of the minister's respect for them. Anyone who genuinely cares can be a warm, active listener.

> I remember vividly the day of my very first counseling session during my internship. It was Monday morning, and I sat in the office nervously trying to recall all I had learned. I had studied many counseling techniques, and I desperately hoped I could recall them. The phone rang, and my ten o'clock appointment was there. She was a woman about 50 years of age. I said, "Hi, my name is Bob Fisher. How can I help you?" At which point, she burst into tears. She started sobbing and began to tell me all the terrible things that had been happening to her. Her husband did not appreciate her.

> Her children were taking advantage of her. She was lonely. She felt abused. She just went on and on. There I sat, worried about being able to say the right thing and do the right thing. But I did not have time to say anything, because she kept pouring out her heart to me. All I did was listen, shake my head, and give her tissues when she needed them. At the end of the hour, as we were wrapping it up, she looked at me and said, "Well, I just want you to know that you have helped me so much in this session today." I had hardly said a word. I only listened to her with compassion and concern.
>
> This was an important lesson for me. On that day in my very first solo counseling session, if I had spent the whole time trying to impress her with my knowledge and all the counseling techniques I had studied, I would have totally missed the point, and she would have benefitted little from it. She needed to talk. She needed to rid herself of these burdens she had been carrying. She needed what psychologists call a catharsis, or a cathartic release. She unburdened herself from all those feelings that she had been carrying. I was there to listen and support her.

When people come to see a minister, they are emotionally starved, discouraged, and probably have nowhere else to go. They need someone who will listen to them, understand their pain, and offer them support. Many times a minister can fill this role better than anyone else.

8 COUNSELING: PART ONE

By Doyle Goff, Ph.D.

Throughout history, there has been a deeply imbedded notion that some individuals are gifted with an ability to assist people who are having problems and difficulties in life. Today, this notion has been institutionalized in a variety of formal helping professions, such as psychiatry, psychology, social work, counseling, and, of course, the ministry. Clergymen are becoming a vital part of the world of counseling. The question is not whether a minister is going to counsel, rather how well counseling will be provided and what the quality of that counseling will be. Ministers are often the first ones to be contacted when people have problems and difficulties. Thus, the minister is in the mainstream of counseling.

What Is Counseling?

Counseling is a means of providing help to people who are making transitions in life. Individuals move from one developmental stage to another—childhood, middle childhood, adolescence, young adulthood, and onward. In each of these stages, difficulties and complex problems are encountered. Occasionally, one is forced to make critical decisions prematurely. Before people are ready, they may be pushed to make decisions on education, career, or marriage. In such stress, related problems can bring people to a point where they cannot function effectively and cannot help themselves. Confronting their problems may require intervention from someone with knowledge of their kinds of issues, and someone who can provide strategies for dealing with the problems.

Stressful problems arise from all kinds of situations and relationships—in one's personal life, in the community, in interaction with others, and with organizations in which one may be involved. Self-doubt, drug addiction, a failing marriage, or the pain of catastrophic loss, may lead people to seek counseling or cause others to encourage them to seek counseling. Some people seek help, not because they are having to manage problems, but to take advantage of the opportunities which life presents to them. In other words, they are not maximizing their potential. Probably, people seek help or intervention from a combination of the two. They are trying to make strides to perform better, to self-actualize, and to become more than they are. The counselor's role is to help people face their problems, deal with life's circumstances, see opportunities for a better life, and maximize their potential.

Characteristics of an Effective Counselor

While it is difficult to determine effective outcomes in counseling, research has provided some clues as to what makes the most effective counselor. For example, if an individual has a problem or concern which he would like to take to a counselor, what type of person would he select? What basic characteristics and qualities would he have? Would these qualities be similar or different to those of his own life? Some adjectives which have been used in literature to describe these qualitites are trustworthy, knowledgeable, caring, warm, nurturing, intelligent, and assertive. Other qualities perhaps come to mind, but these are some of the essential qualitites that help to build a visual image of an effective counselor.

Another attribute which effective counselors possess to a high degree is self-understanding. When one holds unrecognized hostilities, insecurities, strong needs for acceptance, and similar delimiting attitudes, it is important to recognize those challenges in one's personality or thought patterns. Knowing oneself is a prerequisite for understanding others. Personal insight prepares the counselor to understand how people confront the similar issues in their lives.

Psychologist Gary Collins has suggested three ways to achieve better self-understanding.

1. *Reflection.* Reflection means to give time, energy, and the effort to reflect on who one is—do a personal inventory. What are the strengths and the weaknesses?

2. *Identify a friend to confide in.* This person should be someone in whom one has great confidence. Better still, one could seek the help of a professional counselor and discuss these self-revelations.

3. *Invite the Holy Spirit to direct this process.* God knows more about the individual than one will ever know about himself. God is able to shine His search—light of understanding into one's spirit to help him understand the critical issues in his life. Through the Holy Spirit, the Word can reveal one's true self. In fact, while reading Scripture, one might find himself saying, "Ouch, that's hitting home." That is the Word of God, which is sharper than a sword, piercing the spirit and opening to the reader a revelation of himself. At times like these, one can pray with the psalmist: "Search me, O God, and know my heart: try me, and know my thoughts: and see if there be any wicked way in me, and lead me in the way everlasting" (139:23, 24). Barbara Okun believes that it is necessary for counselors to continually assess themselves and their needs. She suggests that counselors ask themselves the following questions:

1. *Am I aware of when I am feeling uncomfortable with a client or with a certain subject area?* The counselor needs to understand areas of content that make them uncomfortable. They need to understand types of people with whom they are not comfortable. One can then take steps to become more comfortable, to become more open and receptive, or discover one's limitations and learn the kinds of situations in which he is best equipped to work.

2. *Am I aware of my avoidance strategies?* The counselor needs to recognize when he is avoiding certain topics. Also, he needs to recognize that when certain topics arise, he feels insecure.

3. *Do I always feel as though I need to be in control of situations?* Effective counselors are not people

who have a strong need for control. The most effective counseling allows people to grow and to change under their own ability and power with the help of God.

4. *Do I become irritated when others do not see things as I do?* Effective counselors are open to thoughts and ideas that differ from their own, and are not irritated by contrary thinking.

5. *Am I so problem-oriented that I'm always looking for the negative and never responding to the positive or the good?* The answer will determine whether one focuses on problems or potentials. One can look at a window, or through a window. To look at the window is to see its marks and imperfections. To look through a window is to see the wonderful world beyond—the outdoors, the trees, the skies, the flowers. The counselor can focus on the window and see only the problems, or look through the window to the potential that lies within the individual. To focus on the good can maximize the potential in the life of the person with whom one is interacting.

Shared Beliefs

An area for consideration in counselor effectiveness is that of shared beliefs. Knowing oneself includes a knowledge of one's beliefs and values. There was a time when people sought to engage in value-free counseling, but there is really no such thing. One cannot come into counseling without bringing his values into the situation. Research shows that effective counselors share some common beliefs and values. *The first shared characteristic of effective counselors is their attitude toward people.* They view people as being able, rather than being unable, as being worthy, rather than unworthy, as being helpful and friendly, rather than hindering and alienating. *Second, effective counselors have a healthy self-concept.* They feel personally adequate, rather than inadequate. They feel that they can identify with others, rather than feel isolated and they feel wanted, rather than unwanted.

The Therapeutic Triad

Carl Rogers talks about the therapeutic triad—factors which need to exist if counselors are to be effective in helping people. Rogers insists that if the therapeutic triad exists, positive change will occur.

1. *Positive regard.* If one communicates acceptance, positive regard is established. If one sees people as worthy, having intrinsic value, positive regard is established.

2. *Genuineness and congruence.* Genuineness means honesty and sincerity in meaning and purpose. When one speaks honestly and acts congruently, the words and actions do not contradict each other; they mesh.

3. *Empathy.* Empathy is like getting inside the skin of the other person, to see the world through his eyes, and feel the pain he feels. Empathy is totally different from sympathy. Sympathy is to feel for someone. Empathy is to feel with someone. The idea of empathy is to walk a mile in the other person's shoes before making any judgments. The concept of empathy is demonstrated by the relationship of parent and infant. Watch the mother and father when they give their baby the first bite of food with a spoon. The parents will prepare for that first bite, pursing their lips, almost trying to eat the food for the infant. That is empathy. In counseling,

empathy builds relationships. It sends a message of respect to the person. Empathy helps one to listen carefully and hear what is really being communicated. It provides support. Empathy puts the counselor on the side of the person who needs help, being for him, not against him. Being for him does not mean that one accepts his behavior. It does not mean that the counselor accepts that individual's attitudes as valid. But it does mean that the counselor supports him and is there for him in his quest to grow and to change. The counselor is nurturing that process. Empathy has been said to lubricate communication—make it flow more smoothly.

Counseling Outcomes

Many purposes have been stated for counseling—both for the counselee and for the counselor. Consider the following:

1. *Effective counselors are freeing rather than controlling.* Their goal is to help free the counselee to grow, to become what he or she needs to become. The goal, then, is releasing or facilitating, rather than controlling and manipulating or coercing.

2. *Effective counselors are self-revealing rather than self-concealing.* They are more open to self-disclosure and transparency than to self-concealment.

3. *Effective counselors are involved rather than alienated.* Helpers tend to be personally involved with those with whom they work, rather than alienated and distant from them.

4. *Effective counselors are more altruistic than narcissistic.* Helpers have an altruistic purpose, a desire to see people better themselves, rather than focusing on their personal needs and their own world. In

other words, successful counselors have an orientation to aiding and assisting other people, rather than attending to personal selfish goals.

5. *Effective counselors have a spiritual dimension in their lives.* First, one needs to be a person of faith. Effective counselors are God-fearing individuals. They are honest. They are readily available. A counselor should be a student who is thoroughly immersed in the Word, familiar with the Word of God, and a follower of Christ, whose very name is Wonderful Counselor.

Counseling Ethics

A final consideration in this lesson is that of ethics. Counseling demands that counselors abide by a code of ethics. Every person who engages in a helping relationship should take a course in ethics and should obtain a code of ethics from a professional organization, whether it be a pastoral counseling organization or an organization such as the American Counseling Association.[1] Every counselor has a responsibility to God, to the people with whom he works, and to the community where he lives.

COUNSELING RESPONSIBILITIES

Here are a few basic principles of counseling ethics.

1. *Always keep confidences.* When individuals reveal private information about their lives, that information must be kept private under any circumstances, excluding legal exceptions. For example,

---

[1]American Counseling Association, 5999 Stevenson Ave., Alexandria, VA 22304-3300.

information regarding child molestation is a reportable offence. But the basic rule of thumb is to keep the confidence of people.

2. *Avoid physical contact.* Apart from a handshake, it is wise to avoid touching a counselee. Sometimes, sexual or other emotional overtones begin at that point. Even though some touching seems harmless and the appropriate social thing to do, it can lead to accusations that place the counselor in serious jeopardy.

3. *Never use the counselee to satisfy your curiosity or sexual desires.* While it may be titillating to receive intensely personal information, this is not beneficial if its foremost purpose is to satisfy the counselor's curiosity.

4. *Do not pressure people to continue counseling.* It is unethical. One can encourage people to get counseling, but the person who does not want help will probably not change in spite of one's best intentions.

5. *Recognize one's own limitations.* Counselors need to recognize that they have limitations. Other than Jesus, who was the perfect counselor, no one has enough understanding and wisdom to help every person with every need. So, one needs to understand his or her limitations and refer people to other professionals—medical doctors, lawyers, or other counselors.

COUNSELING DANGERS

Gary Collins has suggested some dangers in counseling which one should avoid.

1. *Avoid drawing conclusions without hearing the whole matter.* The counselor may need to hear more than one side of a story to keep from drawing

premature conclusions. The Bible admonition to "be swift to hear, slow to speak" (James 1:19) is an appropriate warning.

2. *Do not become involved with the person's problems.* In caring, it is easy to become overinvolved in the problems that people present. Too often, the counselor is tempted to shoulder the problems of other people. When the counselee's problems become the counselor's problems, he has done no good; in fact, he has done harm to himself.

3. *Never use material from a counseling session in a sermon.* Even when names are not called, information spills out that compromises the confidentiality of the session.

4. *Avoid letting counseling take too much of one's own time.* When some ministers get into counseling, they enjoy it so much that it takes up such a huge part of their time that they forget they have been called to other duties.

A Final Word

Those who choose to become involved in a professional way in the field of counseling face a major task. For example, a vast amount of preparation is required to become a licensed professional, and a vast amount of time is required to stay current with the field. To be an effective counselor requires courage. This field is not for people in search of personal gain, affection, or praise. Counseling is a ministry, God-given, to help people realize positive outcomes. If one's reasons are personal and selfish, they will be self-defeating. If one's reasons are not personal and selfish, then that counselor can help meet the needs of the people he serves.

9 COUNSELING: PART TWO

By Doyle Goff, Ph.D.

Several basic skills go into the counseling process. Since the counseling process involves communication between the helper and the client, it is important to focus on relevant communication skills.

Attending Behavior

The first of these skills is attending behavior. Attending means "being with a person—showing that one is present." In the more dramatic moments of life, simply being with another person is very meaningful. Being with that individual in the times of loss and bereavement means much more than words. Helping people through deep interpersonal transactions requires a level of intense attention. The way in which one orients himself physically or psychologically communicates important messages. It says, "I'm with you, I want to hear you." It also puts the counselor in a position to listen carefully to the client's concerns with great detail. By contrast, everyone has had the experience of being ignored during a conversation. For the moment, that person is out there somewhere, but certainly not presently attending to the conversation. The averted face is like having an averted heart. Therefore, anyone in the helping profession should strive to improve his attending skills.

MICROSKILLS

Microskills of attending are basic and most useful. They establish a good, open, friendly environment where clients can share. The acronym **SOLER** can illustrate these small but important skills.

S Squarely
O Open
L Leaning
E Eye contact
R Relax

The **S** stands for squarely—facing the person squarely. A face-to-face posture speaks of being available, wanting to engage, to hear, to understand. The term squarely can be taken literally or metaphorically. The idea is that one's posture is squared with the client. The **O** stands for open—maintain an open posture. The crossing of arms or legs can signal to people that one is closed to them. This is not necessarily the case, but the goal is to communicate to people a sense of openness by the way one attends to them. The question is, To what degree does this behavior say to the person, "I am open to you, and I want to hear you"? The **L** stands for leaning. This means leaning toward a person. When engaged in deep conversation with people, one has a tendency to lean toward them. Again, leaning in their direction suggests attention. Leaning back or away from them is an ultimate form of boredom or disengagement. For example, when one goes to a restaurant and observes two people at a table deep in conversation, he will see that frequently, they lean toward each other. The **E** stands for eye contact. Establishing good eye contact with a person suggests an interest in him and his concerns. This has to be placed in cultural context, because eye contact is a threat in some cultures. But in North America, eye contact is seen as positive affirmation. Good eye contact is the key. Staring can turn people off, but eye contact where one occasionally diverts his gaze maintains a solid connection with the person. The **R** stands for relax. One should be natural and not try to concoct some kind of behavior that will appear artificial. He should be relaxed and natural in his leaning behavior, openness, connectedness, and in attending to people. Establishing good attending behavior produces an environment where people will feel comfortable to talk and to share.

NONVERBAL COMMUNICATION

An effective counselor needs to learn to read his own sensations, feelings, and body reactions. For example, if one feels his muscles tensing as someone talks to him, he can say to himself, *I am feeling anxiety. What is it about this conversation that makes me anxious?* If one can identify the reason for the feeling, this will help to diffuse it. If a client were to say something that instinctively angers the counselor, he can then be aware of his own body language and control the external expression of anger in that situation. Most important, however, is the quality of the counselor's total presence with that client. One's verbal behavior, nonverbal behavior, and the interaction of the two should indicate a willingness to work with an individual.

SOCIAL/EMOTIONAL PRESENCE

The quality of the counselor's total presence with the client is an important factor. Effective counselors stay in touch with how they present themselves, both verbally and nonverbally, but they are not preoccupied with it. To help assess one's presence factor, the following questions can be helpful:

1. What are my attitudes toward this client?
2. How do I rate the quality of my presence with this client?
3. To what degree does my nonverbal behavior indicate a willingness to work with this client?
4. What attitudes am I expressing in my nonverbal behavior? Verbal behavior?
5. To what degree does a client sense that I am effectively working with him?
6. To what degree does my nonverbal behavior reinforce my internal attitudes?
7. In what ways am I distracted from giving my full attention to this client? How will I handle these distractions?

These are questions that relate to social orientation and social-emotional presence.

Listening Skills

Another basic skill in counseling is active listening. One might assume that listening comes naturally and is not a topic needing attention. However, exactly the opposite is true. In the formal school setting, one was taught how to read, write, and speak, but seldom has there been formal instruction in the art of listening—let alone active listening. Listening is seldom taught, and it is hard to do it well.

One listening problem is purely physiological. The average person speaks approximately 125 words a minute. Since one has the capacity to hear in excess of 500 words a minute, this means there is a lot of down time. It is possible to hear what people say and, at the same time, perform other mental functions. Consequently, listening is somewhat casual. It is like going to church, hearing the minister preach, but not really having heard, because while he is speaking, the average person is planning what to do after church or contemplating next week's work. Good counselors cannot do that. They must take the time to focus on context. Excellent counseling focuses on verbal and nonverbal behavior—actively listening to the total person.

One may think he is listening when he can repeat the conversation. But the person still may not feel that he has been heard. That is because he does not feel that he has been attending to him, listening to his emotionality, or listening to the context of the whole message. To be able to repeat a conversation is little more than being a tape recorder. A tape recorder can be plugged in, and play back hours of conversation precisely, but a tape recorder hears nothing. Good listening involves the following four important elements:

1. Observing and reading nonverbal behavior
2. Listening to verbal messages
3. Listening to the context of the message
4. Listening to "sour notes" or difficulties in communication.

Nonverbal Communication

How much nonverbal communication goes on? How much of the message is nonverbal, rather than verbal? The face and the body are extremely communicative—speaking volumes. Two people can be sitting together in silence, but a wide realm of communication can be observed in their nonverbal behavior. One study indicates that when people are looking for cues as to whether or not other people like them, they are looking for nonverbal, as well as verbal messages. Another study indicates that when people are trying to determine whether someone likes them, words contribute only seven percent of that message. Voice cues, vocal inflection and the tone of voice, make up approximately 38 percent of the message, but facial cues account for approximately 55 percent of the message. The exact percentages are not important, but it is accurate to say that a significant portion of communication is nonverbal. And when facial expressions and words do not match—they are not congruent—people tend to believe the nonverbal rather than the verbal. Therefore, it is necessary to focus on what people are saying, nonverbally. It is important to carefully observe body behavior—posture, movements, and gestures. One can learn much by observing facial expressions—smiles, frowns, raised eyebrows, or a turned down mouth. One also hears voice-rated behavior, such as the tone of voice, the pitch of the voice, voice level, and voice intensity. Other observable autonomic physiological responses are breathing rate, a flushed face, a temporary rash, paleness, blushing, pupil dilation, and so forth. One can also look at physical characteristics such as height, fit- ness, weight, grooming, and dress and learn from those attributes. They speak volumes.

This might be termed "listening" to nonverbal behavior. Nonverbal behavior can serve an unspoken but important role similar to that of punctuation in the written word. In addition to being a channel of communication, nonverbal behavior can punctuate a message the same way that periods, commas, and exclamation marks punctuate a written message. They can confirm or repeat a message, giving insight into what the person says or intends to say. Nonverbal cues also can deny or confuse communication. People may say that everything is fine, but if they are crying, everything is not fine. Crying is not congruent with "nothing is wrong" or "everything is OK." When people talk about being calm and relaxed, yet they are shredding the tissues in their hands, the verbal message is not congruent with the nonverbal message.

These messages can mean a host of things, and too much emphasis should not be given to any one message. The key is to look for markers and indicators that are confirmed by other messages. This means taking all communication in context. Verbal messages can mean a wide variety of things. So, how does one tell what meanings are important or which meanings are real? This can be accomplished only by contextualizing the messages. Effective helpers listen patiently to the entire context and try to decipher from that what is meaningful. They refuse to be seduced or overwhelmed by nonverbal messages that lead to hasty conclusions. The total context provides the only path to safe conclusions.

Verbal Messages

Obviously, people speak and communicate, and one has to hear them. People tend to talk about three areas of their lives: experiences, feelings, and behaviors. People tend to talk about experiences most easily. So, when the counselor first sits down with someone, he is very likely to talk about his experiences. Next, he is most comfortable talking about his feelings. The client tends to be least comfortable and is least likely to talk about specific behaviors.

People enjoy talking about their experiences—telling their stories. The client wants to talk about his health, his spouse, his family, and the problems related to these areas of life. The implication is that other people are to blame for his problems, and relating these experiences is often a way to blame someone else for the problems he has experienced. One reason that people need counseling is because they see themselves as victims, adversely affected by other people. They are blaming the immediate social setting or society in its larger context for somehow adversely impacting them. Therefore, they talk extensively about their experiences. For example, company policy discriminates against women; the economy is lousy and there are no jobs; no innovative teacher could ever get ahead in that place. Constant talk about negative experiences is a way of avoiding responsibility. An interesting book entitled *A Nation of Victims* by Sykes, addresses how people in the United States have become whiners, unwilling to take responsibility for their actions. Hence, a school employee who is late every day for months and is fired, sues for reinstatement because chronic tardiness is a disability. Or a woman in McDonald's takes a cup of coffee, spills it in her lap, and sues the restaurant because the coffee is too hot. So, when people talk about life, they often talk about experiences to avoid responsibility.

People talk about their behavior, but this is the area they probably are least likely to talk about. However, people should be encouraged to talk about these areas, because this establishes accountability for experiences. People do things that cause them trouble, and they fail to do things that can get them out of trouble. When these behaviors are discussed, people have to recognize a level of responsibility for those behaviors. People also like to discuss life experiences related to feelings or emotions. The feelings or emotions that flow from their behaviors or from their experiences can be important messages. People also repress or deny their feelings. The effective counselor must listen intently in order to sense the emotion behind the words and attempt to determine if those feelings are congruent with the verbalizations.

The effective counselor must also be a tough-minded listener. Sometimes, perceptions and words are distorted. For instance, if a person sees herself as ugly, when in reality she is beautiful, her experience of seeing herself as ugly is real and needs to be listened to and understood as an experience, even though reality does not square with her perception. The wise counselor hears the sour notes. Tough-minded listeners spot the incongruencies, but reality cannot be ignored forever. At some point, these distortions will need to be confronted.

Habits to Avoid

INADEQUTE LISTENING

Everyone has a problem of inadequate listening. It is easy to be distracted. One may become so involved in his own thoughts that he does not even hear what other people say. One such example is a group of four or five people who are in a circle talking about something. If one stops and analyzes what these people are doing mentally, he will note that in all probability they are formulating their next comment—what they are going to say when their turn comes, rather than listening to what is being said.

EVALUATIVE LISTENING

People also do evaluative listening, which is another shadow side. Even when one listens intently, he often does so with strong evaluation—judging the merits of something. People tend to assess right and wrong, good and bad. While a skilled listener is able to delay that process, he does not want to be so involved in evaluative listening that he misses what people are saying, or he does not hear what they are saying at a depth level.

FILTERED LISTENING

People also do filtered listening. Everyone has biases from his culture and upbringing. The stronger the cultural filters, the greater the likelihood of a bias. And then one uses labels as filters. When a label is placed on someone, the tendency is to listen to people through that label.

FACT-CENTERED LISTENING

Some helpers do informational counseling, posing one question after the other to get more facts. It is entirely possible to collect a wealth of factual information and miss the person altogether. One can fire a barrage of questions and get a host of facts, but have no useful counseling data. The antidote is to listen contextually and focus on the themes and issues that people are really saying verbally and nonverbally.

Beginning counselors may be so concerned about doing the right thing that they spend their time rehearsing what to say next. Sometimes, they do not even listen. They are just trying to think of a good response; for example, what next series of questions would be best. When this happens, they are not listening. They are not hearing people. The clients have been turned off, and they are not able to share the depths of their lives and the depths of meaning that they have brought to the counseling situation.

Communicating effectively is not an easy task. It takes practice. It is a skill that one must work on. These are some of the basic factors, the basic aspects, of the counseling process. Many good books are available on effective communication and listening strategies. Wherever one finds himself, he should practice effective attending and listening skills. It will certainly make counseling significantly more effective.

10 CONFLICT RESOLUTION: PART ONE

By Paul Conn, Ph.D.

To this point, this study has examined several aspects of human development and behavior with implications for ministry. This chapter will look at one of the most important aspects of ministerial behavior—coping with conflict and conflict resolution.

The Ministry and Conflict

In the real world, everything does not always go well; everyone is not happy with everyone else; there is bad news, as well as good; troubled waters, as well as smooth. This not only characterizes the world of today, but also the spiritual life and the ministerial world as well. Few ministers fail because of their inability to deal with success. Typically, failure in ministry results from an inability to deal with problems and face decline. When there are no difficulties, one can function somewhat instinctually. But when conflict develops, the core ingredient to maintaining leadership in ministry often is in knowing how to cope with conflict and how to resolve it. Resolving conflicts, like every other aspect of human behavior, is not the exclusive concern of psychologists. Scripture addresses conflict as a natural part of the human experience. Conflict, in this sense, is not necessarily physical confrontation. Conflict might mean tension. It might mean ideological confrontation—a clash of wills, a clash of personalities, or the tension created among individuals when opposite agendas are advocated. However, several important principles exist for dealing with conflict.

Five Basic Principles of Conflict Resolution

1. *Conflict is normal and not all conflict is bad.* Some conflict is creative and has positive uses. Conflict frequently issues from conflicting styles, not from any basic difference of values. Jesus seemed to enjoy contrasting styles. Among the 12 original disciples which He attracted to Himself, one can observe very different kinds of people—men whose varied approaches to the work of life frequently brought them into conflict. Their differences were usually not a basic struggle between good and evil, or a conflict between right and wrong, but a clash produced by contrasting styles. That is often the case inside or outside of the church. When that kind of conflict is properly resolved, it is not necessarily bad. It is quite common, and sometimes, it is even very creative.

2. *Good conflict may deepen superficial relationships.* In surface relationships that characterize contemporary life, people may never get close enough even to have conflict. Frequently, disagreements deepen such relationships, if they are properly

resolved. Conflict left to fester and become chronic is rarely positive. When conflict occurs within the body of Christ and it is properly resolved, it can deepen superficial relationships.

3. *Personal growth often occurs through dissonance.* Dissonance simply means a lack of agreement-disagreement. This principle was offered by the Swiss psychologist, Jean Piaget. Piaget's basic assumption was that growth, whether it is intellectual, moral or relational, frequently occurs through dissonance. The social imbalance brought on by trouble urges people to grow in their search for resolution. Within the body of Christ and among men and women of goodwill, conflict is common, not always bad, and can have positive outcomes.

Scripture offers many examples of conflict. There are specific examples of interpersonal conflict in the New Testament—even among the followers of Jesus. The Twelve who were closest to Jesus frequently found themselves in various kinds of conflict with one another. One of the great texts of Scripture comes when the disciples inquired of themselves and Jesus, "Who is the greatest in the kingdom of heaven?" (Matthew 18:1). Each wanted to be closest to the Lord. They found themselves in conflict even in the presence of Jesus. Jesus used their conflict to help them grow.

In his conflict with the Judaizers, Paul spoke to Peter about the problem in a very confrontational tone (Galatians 2:11-14). There was a significant conflict between these two great men. The question is, Was either of these men in the flesh or outside the range of Christ's teaching? They were not. Both were good men, led of the Holy Spirit, who found themselves in conflict over the issue of freedom from the Jewish law. A careful reading of the Galatians passage reveals the depth of this sharp conflict between two leaders in the early church community.

Another type of conflict happened between Paul and Barnabas. In Acts 15, the issue of John Mark's value to their missionary travels shows a marked difference of opinion. The question at issue was whether John Mark should be ostracized and abandoned as a colleague in ministry because of his earlier failings. Clearly, Paul and Barnabas clashed over the role of John Mark.

At various places in the teachings of Christ, important lessons emerge from conflict. One of those is that most loved parable of the Prodigal Son. The core teaching of this parable is the lost condition of the son and the father's willingness to forgive him and embrace him again as his son. Another theme, is the conflict between the prodigal son and the brother who stayed at home. Jesus talked about the conflict within this family as a way of giving a larger lesson. Also, in the work of Christ himself, a conflict arose between Jesus and the outsiders in the government over the issue of taxes. When Jesus discussed the issue of taxes, conflict clearly existed.

Resolving conflict within the community of faith requires a commitment to the body of Christ. If one does not have a commitment to the body of Christ, then one does not have a commitment to resolving conflict within that body. If people have such a low threshold for conflict within the body of Christ that they abandon it because there is conflict, the body of Christ and the church will be constantly fragmented. If one loses confidence in the value of the body because of people in the body they do not like, or people in the body who misuse others, or simply because conflict emerges in the body, then the whole family of faith falls apart. Conflict in the church and in the ministry must be approached with a bottom-line commitment to the body of Christ. That commitment must be this: Involvement is worth the effort, worth the pain, and worth the work it takes to solve conflict within the body of Christ. In some secular relationships, one has the freedom to walk away from confrontation that might lead to a conflicting situation. For example, if one goes to a store and has an argument with the cashier, he just never has to go to that store again. Sometimes in one's ordinary, everyday life, the best way to avoid continuing conflict is to walk away from the situation or walk away from the individual when conflict arises. But the freedom to walk away is not available within the church. In the church, one has a responsibility to deal with conflict rather than abandon people over a conflict, or abandon the situation because conflict arises. Overcoming trouble in the community of faith requires a commitment to the body of Christ.

4. *A model of advocacy may appear to be contention when it is not really conflict.* Advocacy is an effective way to reach decisions. At Lee University there exists an advocacy model involving the major decision makers. The five vice-presidents meet regularly with the president to present conflicting or contrasting ideas and approaches about what needs to be done. The model is that everyone may strongly advocate his or her point of view, and a decision is reached after vigorous debate of the varying views that are offered and advocated. At the end, there is resolution and peace, but in the middle of

the discussion, it may look like mortal combat. It is not conflict. It is advocacy.

In the church and in the ministry, room must be given for advocacy. Men and women who are intelligent, God-fearing, Spirit-filled, Christ-centered individuals can advocate different points of view, stay at the table and stay within the body of Christ as they resolve their differences. What appears to be conflict, can be just a very good decision-making model.

5. *There is a biblical pattern for resolving conflict.* Matthew 18:15,16, gives a pattern for resolving conflict. "If your brother sins against you, go and show him his fault, just between the two of you. If he listens to you, you have won your brother over. But if he will not listen, take one or two others along, so that every matter may be established by the testimony of two or three witnesses" (NIV). This excellent approach to resolving most conflict comes directly from the teaching of Jesus.

Five Basic Causes of Conflict

1. *Conflict is frequently caused by unmatched expectations.* Unmatched expectations can lead to disappointment which leads to loss of confidence. Conflict in the church often arises from a misunderstanding about what to expect. A different set of expectations is almost a certain recipe for conflict.For example, if a choir member expects to sing a solo, is primed for the task, and has family present to hear the solo, but the choir director has not planned to use that person as a soloist, and it does not happen, this probably will lead to conflict. Then the pastor finds himself sorting out the problem between the minister of music and the family within the

church because they were not together on exactly what to expect. When a visiting minister goes into a church to be a guest speaker, a certain amount of time is given for the sermon. If the pastor expects the visiting minister to take a different amount of time, that expectation sows the seeds of potential conflict. Most of the time when conflict happens, expectations are not matched and are not met.

2. *Conflict is caused by the mounting number of buried hurts, slights, and insults.* Like green stamps or frequent flyer points, they are kept, added together, and cashed in for something. Burying disappointments, personal injuries, and negative experiences is a most deadly illness in the body of Christ. This is not to suggest that it is psychologically healthy to always go around venting one's problems, but it is definitely psychologically unhealthy and spiritually inadvisable to bury one's hurts. At some point, one has to give things to the Lord and then give them up. To carry them around until finally they become like a cancer, is what the Scripture means when it refers to a growing root of bitterness. Conflict between two people or between an individual and a larger group of people in the church grows from a gradual buildup of hurt and disappointment.

3. *A major cause of conflict is unexpressed fears.* People may find themselves resisting others because of fears that have never been expressed. At Lee University, one of the department faculties was in conflict with some of the university leadership over what they feared might occur. The conflict was found to be unnecessary and the conflict easily resolved when the fears were expressed. It is easy to become paranoid in the church. It is easy to be

fearful about what might happen in situations involving other Christians. When these fears are not expressed, they can never be countered, they can never be checked out, and they can never be resolved.

4. *Competition for limited resources can cause conflict.* There is never enough money, time, and attention in the work of the Lord. A pastor or minister is placed in many situations within the church where there is competition for time, attention, and financial resources. A leader must respond by constantly reassuring people in an atmosphere of fairness so that conflict does not issue from a feeling they can never get the appropriate time, attention, or resources. The feeling that "I'm not valued as highly as someone else within the body of Christ" is another certain recipe for trouble.

5. *Conflict escalates in a hostile and failing environment.* Psychological studies show that if people or animals are put in situations in which pain is delivered and discomfort created, individuals or animals will always turn against one another and start fighting. Original studies in this area were done with rats placed in a small box in which they were shocked periodically and where there was nothing they could do to escape the shock. They were not shocked for any particular reason. They were just shocked randomly. If two rats are put in a box and constantly shocked, the two rats will begin to fight one another even though fighting one another does not turn off the shock or solve the problem. Studies indicate that if an individual is in a hostile or a negative environment, the person will frequently respond to that environment in a rather illogical way by creating conflict with others in that

environment. For example, members of a losing ball team have trouble getting along.

When a church is shrinking and things are not going well, conflict seems to grow. When a revival is not going well, people are not coming to the services, and no one is coming to the Lord, it becomes easier for the "blame game" to start and for conflict to begin. The cause of the conflict may be simple. In a hostile environment without really understanding why they do it, or without meaning it personally, individuals may strike out and lash out at other people.

When Conflict Needs Attention

As previously noted, conflict may be positive and constructive, or at times, conflict is neither positive nor negative—it is just there. How does one know when conflict is out of line? What guidelines can be used to determine whether conflict is a problem that needs attention or a condition to be tolerated and observed?

1. *Conflict is out of line if it inhibits those involved from participation in the life of the church.* If a conflict, for whatever reason, stops people from pursuing the things of God, it is a bad situation. Ministers respond to conflict with various degrees of aggressiveness. Some will stamp it out every time they see it. Others tend to let it work itself out. Value exists in both approaches, but conflict is unacceptable if it keeps either of the combatants or parties involved from doing the work of the Lord.

The practice of footwashing was placed in the church by our Lord as a means of self-examination in times of conflict. While there is no magic in washing another man or woman's feet, it is a gesture, a sacrament, placed in the body of Christ by the Lord because He understood the sensitive implications of this simple behavior—a reflection of feelings and attitudes toward each other. It is a place to check oneself. When one is unwilling to wash another person's feet or to have a person wash his or her feet because of tension or conflict with that person, that conflict is destructive. If one is even uncomfortable with the idea, the conflict is probably injurious to the body of Christ. When it is difficult to make an expression of affection or love to a brother or sister in the body of Christ, the conflict itself probably needs to be resolved. If the conflict with another individual makes it hard to seek the Lord on his or her behalf, the conflict is probably out of line.

2. *When conflict damages the witness of the church, it needs resolution.* The Scripture teaches that "By this shall all men know that ye are my disciples, if ye have love one to another" (John 13:35). When conflict is so great that it spills over to the outside world and damages the witness of the church, somebody in a position of ministerial leadership needs to do something about it.

3. *When conflict distracts from the larger task of the church, it needs resolution.* Occasionally, Lee University has critics. The University is frequently second-guessed on the many difficult judgment calls made about student behavior, worship practices, or what is taught. A few years ago, a very outspoken minister, who is no longer in the denomination, became so hostile toward Lee University that the conflict reached the point of occupying too much time and attention. Criticism within the body of Christ is not necessarily a nonspiritual act if done properly—in

love and in a constructive manner. However, when criticism congeals into true, chronic conflict, and people find themselves distracted from the mission of winning the lost and building the kingdom because they are investing so much psychic and spiritual energy in the conflict, that is a sure sign that the conflict needs attention.

4. *When conflict is along vertical lines of spiritual authority, it is wrong and needs attention.* The Scripture clearly teaches obedience to those in authority. An outstanding pastor spoke these words to a group of young, ministerial students at Lee University:

> As an associate pastor, the single most important lesson I learned was this. Anytime the senior pastor takes a position of principle, I have two simple responses to make—either "Yes, sir" or "I resign." It is not a biblical option to stay and be in conflict with the person who is over you in the Lord.

If conflict occurs along vertical lines of spiritual authority and is chronic and ongoing, it is negative, and it is wrong.

11 CONFLICT RESOLUTION: PART TWO

By Paul Conn, Ph.D.

This course has looked at various principles which teach about the human experience, both from Scripture and from the literature of psychology. An interest in human experience is important, not just because of the importance to oneself, but because the believer cares about ministry, and ministry necessarily involves other people. Effective ministry is not based just on one's knowledge of God, but it must include one's knowledge of the people who are the object of God's redemptive plan. Thus, an attempt to understand oneself and others implies that one must examine the human side of the equation of God plus man.

Conflict is a dominant feature of the human experience. In fact, conflict pervades all human relationships both inside and outside of the church. In many ways, successful ministers are conflict-management specialists. In the rub of ordinary life, in the work of all ministers, one must learn how to respond to conflict or it will impede the flow of the Holy Spirit in the lives of the congregation. This chapter addresses the qualities that are required to resolve conflict and become skilled "peacemakers."

Essential Qualities for Conflict Resolution

1. *An attitude that harmony is important.* That means that one must care about resolving conflict. One way of responding to trouble among people in the congregation or trouble between oneself and others is just to ignore it and hope that it will go away. There is a tendency to accept the idea that it is going to happen; therefore, not very much can be done about it. That is not an appropriate attitude for a minister or even a Christian leader at the lay level. Once it is determined that negative or destructive conflict exists, harmony must become the goal of the leader. This is a valid principle even in the secular world.

Based on the pragmatic principle of efficiency—friction creates heat—something must be done to change the situation. If friction creates loss of efficiency in machines, the principle is even more valid in the spiritual world. When conflict is ignored in the spiritual realm, the cost is even greater, because harmony is the oil that reduces friction and produces an atmosphere for spiritual growth. The presence of harmonious and pleasant association creates the positive climate that engenders body life in the spiritual realm. Tremendous energy and power are created when men and women who share the same Lord and the same faith in harmonious relationship, come together in unity of purpose. The church needs to learn to spot conflict, deal with it early, and emphatically root it out. Such an approach to conflict resolution releases the power of harmony within the body of Christ.

Some management specialists and leaders within the secular community teach that conflict is advantageous, because when people are set against one another, competition increases productivity. That attitude should not to be transported to the life of the church. Whereas the church has to make certain concessions to the natural human experience of competition and to the occasional conflict that arises from it, the church ought never to capitulate to competition as the natural mode of life in the church. Cooperation is the natural mode of life in the church. Harmony is the natural state of the church and enlightened leadership has to be committed to that harmony.

Many possibilities flow from a community that is harmonious which are not possible in isolated, individual expressions of discipleship. First, there is warmth in the body of Christ when that body of believers live harmoniously together and more closely together. That warmth is never available to anyone who is isolated and alone. Every Christian needs the warmth of other people. While people may get accustomed to living without relationships, they suffer immense loss by living in isolation.

There is also strength in harmony. A single strand of thread has some strength, but with a second, third, and fourth strand, those several chords bound together have geometrically greater strength than any one of them separately. People are stronger when they come together. In harmony with brothers and sisters, the believer finds strength.

Not only is there warmth and strength in harmony, there is greater range. Together, people have the ability to spread the gospel further. Greater warmth, greater strength, and greater range, come from harmonious relationships, but commitment to harmony means taking risks.

2. *A willingness to communicate openly, effectively and constructively.* It is much easier not to say what is really meant, if one thinks that what he really means might not be well received. It is much easier to be closed if one fears that he might be embarrassed—singled out and ridiculed—by telling what is really on his mind. But in the body of Christ, there must be a commitment to open communication. Much of the conflict in the church simply comes from an unwillingness to engage in open expression with one another—to express the love one feels, the disagreements, and the fears.

3. *The ability to take another person's perspective.* This is considered so important among psychologists that the field of role playing and role reversal has been developed as a psychological technique, teaching people to accept the perspective of another person.

> As a young psychologist working as a counselor, I was called upon to counsel with a teenager who was in conflict with his father. This was a typical Christian family. The son, a fine young man, and the father, a Christian leader, both loved the Lord. They found themselves in conflict over a simple matter. The son did not want to play tennis with his father. That may sound trivial, but since the dad wanted to play tennis with his son, and the son never wanted to play tennis with his dad, a conflict had been created that grew into a serious problem between father and son. They came to me because they both understood that the issue was much more important than playing tennis.

> I asked this young man to pretend that he was the dad, and let me play the role of the son. In a series of counseling sessions, the son enjoyed being the dad and speaking with paternal authority. After a few role reversal sessions, the young man started to gain insight into how his father must feel. I then suggested that he start to play tennis with his father. This suggestion forced him to recall the feelings he experienced while pretending to be the father. He began playing tennis with his dad, and the result was an improved communication. Over the next few months, their relationship flowered into a wonderfully healed bonding between father and son. In this case, healing a growing breach over something as unimportant as a tennis game depended on the son understanding the father's feelings.

Seeing the other person's point of view is a key to resolving conflict.

4. *An ability to detach emotion from issues.* It is not easy to take the feeling out of an issue that produces conflict and approach it reasonably and without emotion. It may take time to detach emotion from the issue and be able to approach the problem with logic and reason, but in the heat of conflict, the delay of confrontation and taking time to think clearly is a wise decision. The Scripture offers this advice: "My dear brothers, take note of this: Everyone should be quick to listen, slow to speak and slow to become angry" (James 1:19 NIV). Sometimes the healing process has to be slowed down because time can drain the emotion out of the conflict and let logic preside. It is easier to resolve logical conflict than it is to resolve emotional conflict—easier to see clearly the reasoning of a particular issue than to sort through conflict that takes on a strong emotional tone.

5. *The ability to understand that conflict is not necessarily or essentially competitive.* There does not always have to be a winner and a loser in every conflict. Frequently, a competitive instinct keeps people from resolving their conflicts with others. Locked in a disagreement, the natural tendency is to refuse to concede, because losing the argument seems to surrender the higher ground or the greater advantage. When one understands that conflict is not necessarily competitive, that there is not necessarily a winner or a loser, it allows movement toward resolution.

In the course of enlarging Lee University, the campus experienced great expansion over a period of a dozen years. To expand the physical facilities, the University acquired many small parcels of property around the perimeter. During this 12-year-period, 105 houses were acquired and bull- dozed on our immediate perimeter. This rapid property acquisition placed the University in a situation where it was necessary to deal with predatory people who bought property because they thought it might be profitable. Someone might buy a piece of property for $30 thousand and attempt to sell it to the University for $75 thousand. This had the potential of placing the University in conflict with these individuals over property prices.

One of the big problems was the president's competitive spirit. I tended to get locked into a struggle because I did not want a predator to win this tug of war. In short, I did not want to lose. My view was that people were ripping off the school and forcing me to surrender larger amounts of money that was badly needed by the University. Ultimately, I found that I had to

> back way off and realize that I was in personal com- bat with these people about winning and losing, but the issue was not about that. Our goal was to get the property. They had it and we needed it. My one challenge was to come up with the money so we could buy the property and build our building. If I got it in my mind that these people were in a competition with me, and unfairly gaining an advantage over me, that mind-set made it impossible to resolve the issue and move on.

That is often the case in the contests and tensions that arise within a church.

Avoiding the Roadblocks

Some behaviors are roadblocks to successful resolution of conflict. The terms used to describe nonconstructive ways of coping are the psychologist's way of describing an attitude or posture that characterizes nonproductive attempts at problem solving. These eight roadblocks always get in the way of resolving conflict.

1. *Denial of conflict and anger.* This is a simple mechanism in which an individual acts as if there is no conflict—no anger, no negative feeling. The problem has been pushed underground and is being denied. Psychologists sometimes refer to this as a defense mechanism and identify it as repression. Repression is simply to push negative feelings out of mind. No one in the church wants to admit they are hostile or angry, and a tendency to fake it and assume a "feel good" attitude in the church frequently stands in the way of resolving the actual conflict. Counselors, who spend time dealing with the emotional problems of Christians, find repressed anger and hostility within the church to be

a serious problem. In an eagerness to please God, people simply deny their negative feelings, but God is neither pleased nor honored with this. While one should not advertise negative feelings or hold them up for all to see, one should be able to recognize and admit his or her feelings. The Scripture speaks of knowing oneself and looking into his own heart. The psalmist prays: "[Lord], see if there be any wicked way in me" (139:24). This is an acknowledgment that believers are not always honest with themselves about negative feelings. When personal combat is on, it is likely that long-denied, repressed feelings are pushing the agenda and fueling the war. When people are in constant disagreement with one another, this quarrel probably issues from some sort of long-held, negative feelings. Denial of negative feelings and the anger that accompanies it, stands in the way of dealing with conflict and is counterproductive to resolution.

2. *Overcompensation for negative attitudes by overdoing it.* People who "overdo it" virtually ooze with sweetness. They tend to be so afraid of hurting others that they do not ever give other people bad news. They are so apprehensive about creating trouble or disturbing the harmony in the body that they are unwilling to express even the slightest disagreement. They overcompensate for their negative feelings by assuming a kind of phony piety, which exacerbates rather than solves the problem.

3. *Passive hostility.* One does not have to throw sand in the gears to slow things down. Psychologists find that people who are chronically late, who are constantly bringing up trivial objections, who somehow find reasons not to go along with the agenda of the group, are frequently just pas-

sively hostile. They are getting even by doing nothing. They may think that they are cleverly winning a point by subtly resisting the other person, but sadly, they are not dealing with the problem—the hostility and anger they really feel.

4. *A general irritability.* Some people are just mad at the world. Actually, they are mad at something specific in the world, some person particularly in the world, but it comes out as a kind of generalized irritability which can appear at any time over any situation.

5. *Letting things build up-the last straw phenomenon.* Some final small thing happens and this person finally blows up.

> There was a staff person at Lee University who worked very hard, never expressed any real disagreement or unhappiness with any particular situation, until a small event happened here at the institution and he just blew, walked out—left. Why this man would suddenly resign and express so much negative emotion over such a trivial matter was a mystery. A careful study of the incident revealed that no one small thing had precipitated the stunning negative reaction. Rather, there had been a buildup of one thing after another that had not been handled, until finally, he experienced the "last straw" phenomenon, resulting in the big blowup.

6. *A generalized or free-floating anxiety.* When people become unhappy, they may be fearful and anxious in many different situations. Frequently, the basis for this anxiety is unresolved conflict in their lives.

7. *Signs of psychosomatic illness.* Constant headaches, lower back pain, ulcers, and heart problems, may come from internalizing conflict rather than dealing with it and resolving it.

8. *Overreacting and pressing the fight with everyone.* These people never suppress conflict. They are ready to fight over every little thing.

One might ask whether these are problems which Christians encounter. Of course, they are. Being children of God and being filled with the Holy Spirit does not prevent people from experiencing these personality problems. Fear, anxiety, depression, or exhaustion can be experienced by devout people. God made man and woman to be the temple of the Holy Spirit, and when the laws of nature are violated or ignored, one pays a price for it. This wonderfully crafted organism which God created requires the believer to pay attention to these warning signs.

Qualities of the Peacemaker

The question presents itself, "Would I make a good peacemaker?" The discussion of conflict leads naturally to this question as it relates to each one. In the familiar Sermon on the Mount, Jesus said, "Blessed are the peacemakers: for they shall be called the children of God" (Matthew 5:9). What about the believer? Does he see himself as a peacemaker in those areas of life in which he finds conflict? What are the salient qualities of a good peacemaker?

1. *Credibility.* People on both sides of the conflict have to trust the peacemaker. Two failures interfere with one's role as a credible peacemaker. One is a lack of impartiality. The other is a lack of confidentiality. If one is going to step in the middle between

two church members, two pastors, or two family members, the ability to be viewed as impartial is critical. It is equally important to treat the sensitive conversations that inevitably emerge in conflict situations as confidential information. People must believe that the peacemaker really listens carefully, giving an honest hearing to both parties, and that he will not spread everything he hears. At the heart of peacemaking is a person who will listen carefully as someone unloads the emotion of a conflicting situation, and who can be trusted not to go tell what he hears. Everyone needs a friend to whom he can say, "Just let me vent and forget this after I say it." These qualities make a good peacemaker.

2. *Spiritual vitality.* Being a peacemaker in the church is a ministry that can never be done entirely in one's own strength—the flesh. One who enters a conflict-laden situation without a robust spiritual vitality, may become a victim of the conflict. A peacemaker must be connected to the Prince of Peace. Peacemakers must serve in the power of the Holy Spirit with spiritual vitality flowing through them, or they may wind up in the ditch, wrestling with the combatants.

3. *Caring.* Not everyone cares enough to be a peacemaker.

> I am an academic psychologist in addition to being a minister, and before I became president of Lee University, I was a psychology professor. Human behavior is fascinating. I love to analyze it, to think about it, and to read about it. I respect it. In my early years of preparation as a psychologist, I thought I needed to become a counselor so I could help people with their problems. One of the most positive things that ever happened to me professionally was when

> Jim Mowry, a born-again psychiatrist at the Atlanta Counseling Center, talked to me about counseling. He pointed out that I did not care enough about other people's problems to be a good clinical psychiatrist or a good counselor. This was shocking to me, but it was true. So, I pursued the study of academic psychology. I am not a bad guy, but I do not have the qualities of empathy and caring that make me a person who would be happy spending my days helping other people solve their problems. You might not either, and if you do not, it is a good thing to know about yourself.

People have different gifts. Some people have the gift to proclaim, some the gift to teach, some the gift to serve, and others the gift to care. Whoever would be a peacemaker needs to possess a gift of caring.

4. *Vulnerability.* To be a peacemaker, one becomes vulnerable to the risk of undeserved blame because people in conflict frequently lash out at peacemakers. It is an old cliche that where two people are fighting and a third person moves in to stop the fight, the third party winds up getting punched out. This is just as true in church fights. If one wants to be a peacemaker, he must be willing to be vulnerable to hurt. People in conflict will almost always lash out at whoever is trying to resolve the conflict.

5. *The ability to be comfortable with conflict.* Sometimes, a peacemaker has to tolerate life with tension. It is important to slowly work through difficulty rather than rushing to a speedy but imperfect solution. Living comfortably with dissonance in the tension of conflict, while solutions slowly emerge, is the sign of a good peacemaker. Some people are

so nonconfrontational, so unwilling to live with this kind of tension, that they do not function well in these situations. Opting for the false calm of quick solutions like "kiss and make up" or "shake hands and be friends," they never really deal with the problem. This is not the mark of a good peacemaker.

6. *Availability.* This means dedicating one's time to the effort. If one is a busy person dealing with numerous operational issues, he may not have the freedom to make himself available to the sensitive task of conflict resolution.

7. *The ability to humanize the conflict.* To humanize conflict is to take the issues out of the theoretical or the abstract and make them real. The causes of conflict are personal and are adversely impacting the lives of real people. They should not be viewed as impersonal ideas or treated as theoretical constructs.

8. *An ability to facilitate communication—to get other people to talk.* This skill starts with listening attentively. It continues with getting people to be honest and open in what they are saying. As this kind of dialogue occurs, the Word of God can be applied to their situations.

Conflict is in the church, because human beings are in the church. To truly understand the work of God, one must understand how to deal with the tensions that arise. To have an effective ministry in this area, it would be wise to diligently seek the Lord while searching for the best books and finest training in conflict and conflict resolution.

12 DEVELOPING CHRISTIAN FAMILIES

By Paul Conn, Ph.D.

The impact of family-related problems on a church, as well as in the minister's personal life, underscores the importance of the study of family relationships, especially for ministers. As a ministry expands, family-related issues in the church require significantly more of the pastor's time, but the minister's primary responsibility continues to be the children whom God has placed in his or her own family. Perhaps, there is no greater tragedy than to minister the love and the grace of Jesus Christ to other people's sons and daughters, but not to be able to see that grace expressed in one's own children. As imperfect fathers and mothers, ministers face the same challenges and experience the same successes and failures in child rearing as other families in the church. Pastors confront the same family dynamics and cope with the same formidable tasks in rearing their children as anyone in their congregation.

Myths About Parenting

There are many erroneous ideas about the family life of ministers. Some of these myths are prevalent and widely accepted, but absolutely untrue. The following six myths can be considered as six erroneous conclusions about family life for ministers.

1. *Quality time makes up for quantity time in one's home life.* In this busy world, it is assumed the lack of time can be replaced by more intense activity. So, the concept of quality time has developed as a remedy for parents who stay too busy to spend the time with their children that good parenting requires. The result is that hard-working ministers and their wives, who sometimes also have careers that take them away from their families, are consoled with the idea that while the quantity of time may not be there, the quality is there.

It is a myth to assume that in the time spent with one's children, quality can make up for quantity. This is about as logical as saying, "I don't have very much food to give the children, but I have high-quality food." A steak can be of superb quality, cut from the world's finest beef—succulent, tender and juicy—but if it is only the size of a postage stamp, it will not provide the necessary nutrition to keep someone healthy and alive. High quality just does not make up for lack of quantity. That is true in assessing time one spends with the family. To minister is to serve. This consumes one's attention, time and energy. While fulfilling the role of God's servant, the minister has to realize that his or her children demand the same quantity of time as the people they serve—not just moments measured in minutes, but time measured in hours.

President Lyndon Johnson's daughter shared this story of her relationship with her father. Shortly before he died, the president apologized to her for his failings as a father. The daughter, wanting to make him feel better, protested by suggesting that he had been a great father. Once, she told him, he even flew to the football game where she was the homecoming queen. At halftime, his helicopter landed on the 50-yard line. Stepping out of the helicopter, and waving to the crowd, she recalled, he placed the crown on her head before boarding the helicopter and flying away. She said this was a great moment she would remember forever. Then the president said, "Yes, I know honey. You're right. I was there for the big moments. But I'm apologizing for being such a poor dad because I was never there for the small moments."

That is what all children need from their dads. They do not need super preachers who are wonderful to everyone but them and accessible to everyone but them and always missing the little moments. The most vital relationships between parents and their children are developed in the small day-to-day moments, when they spend quantity time, as well as quality time, with their children.

2. *If I do everything right, my children will turn out right.* The Scripture does say, "Train up a child in the way he should go: and when he is old, he will not depart from it" (Proverbs 22:6). But this is a statement of relationship, not an iron-clad guarantee that children will make the right decisions and experience no pain in the process. On the contrary, they have to find their own way and make their own mistakes. God gives the freedom to choose, and one's independent decisions prevail, regardless if he is 15

or 50. Parents cannot make things turn out right for their children and make them want to serve God simply by making all the right moves and being the perfect parents. Ultimately, the lives they live are their own choices.

> I had wonderful Christian parents. My father has been a minister for almost 60 years. My mother was a godly woman, and a great mother. They had 12 children, and among those 12 children, there has been much pain. I look at our individual development, the way each of the 12 of us approached our own lives, and I see the contrasts, the way we chose different paths, as God brought us to where He wanted us to be or where we chose to be. At some point in life, that gets beyond the reach of even the most godly parents.

One does what he can and then he must leave the rest to God. It does not matter if the parents make all the right moves, their child still will experience suffering and pain, and will choose his or her own path in life.

3. *You can't help a hurting person if you are hurting.* It is not true that one must be perfect or almost perfect to help other people. One of the great lessons in Scripture comes from Mark where a man came to Jesus for healing and Jesus asked him, "Do you believe?" This was his answer. "Lord, I believe; help my unbelief" (9:24 NKJV). He was trying to believe. He wanted to believe. He hoped he believed. He thought he believed, but part of him still had doubts, so he said, "Help my unbelief." Here was a person, troubled by doubt, who held on to some of his faith and God honored it.

At times, people fail to reach out to their children and minister the grace of God to them because they are sharply aware of their own weaknesses and imperfections. They have doubts, and they flinch from forcefully affirming their faith to their children. But children need to hear their parents express their faith to them even when they have doubts. Children need a model, an image, and a vision of Jesus Christ even in the darkest hour.

> Looking back to my own childhood, I now see times when my parents encountered challenges and had doubts about direction. Even in those times, they consistently and reliably communicated to me a vision of hope, optimism, and faith. Even when they experienced trouble and pain, they inspired me with their faith and confidence.

4. *Once a family starts to fall apart, it is all over.* Ministers and their wives sometimes give up too early on their children. They tend to believe the worst too quickly, and lose their confidence, their optimism, and their faith in their children. When trouble comes and the family starts to fall apart, do not give up hope. That is the time to hold on to the promises of God. Many times, a child who grows up in a minister's home will seem to be moving resolutely out of the orbit of his or her parents and out of the direction and the path which they have set for that child. However, this is usually an expression of the child's search for authentic personal faith, not the profound rejection parents fear.

> Working at a Christian college for 28 years, I have had an opportunity to see many troubled students. I have observed the cycle of their

> getting themselves together, finding a sure faith, developing a solid walk with the Lord, and then moving on to serve the church and their own families. If I had the freedom to do so, I could share stories of people—whose names you would recognize because they are now productive and well known in ministry—who, while at Lee University, struggled with their faith and all the implications of growing up in a minister's home. The last chapter has not been written in the life of your child. Some of the most brilliant examples of the grace of God include periods of struggle where parents had nothing to hold to but faith in the redemptive work of Jesus Christ.

Families and children go through cycles. When the children are at home at mother's knee, the bond is close, the children are manageable, and the parents are happy. Then come the stresses of pre-adolescence and adolescence. At college age, the children leave the orbit of parents and explore new ideas, new values and new beliefs. Frequently, it seems, when parents are in what can be described as a down cycle with their children, or when the child is in a period that gives cause to worry, the parents feel a horrible sense of loss. They feel like the earlier days of innocence are lost forever and that sense of closeness, that earlier bonding, can never be regained. Do not believe it. They do grow up, and as they grow up, the pressures increase. Except for the memories, one does lose that earlier period of life with the children, but as they grow, there is a newer, better period ahead. Even when families seem to be falling apart, they are probably just passing through a cycle that will end in triumph. God has been through this with millions of families and brought them out, and He will do it again.

5. *If I can protect my child from pain, I should do so.* This is a myth, because the child has to experience pain to understand its lessons. Some of the greatest growth in life comes from pain.

> When my son was a small child, one Christmas season he wanted to play with the light bulbs on the Christmas tree. My wife's approach was to constantly run over and take him away from the tree, explaining patiently that the lights would burn him. He still wanted to reach out and touch the brightly colored lights. This went on for days until I finally decided to let him touch one. He walked over to the tree, knowing he was not supposed to, and looked over his shoulder to see if his mother would stop him. She did not. He looked at me and I didn't either. So, he reached out and grabbed the light bulb. It was very hot and it burned his little hand. He screamed, he cried, and he rolled on the floor, but he never touched another light bulb. A little pain will be a great teacher for one's children.

Mark Twain once said that a cat, having sat on a hot stove lid, will never again sit on a hot stove lid, nor for that matter, on a cold stove lid. That is a lesson that only the stove lid can teach.

Kevin Leman, talks about what he calls snow plowing the roads of life for one's child. And he says, "So many Christian parents are so determined to keep their children from ever hurting, from ever being in need, that they never hurt and they are never in need until finally they run outside of their parent's care and they are totally unprepared for challenge and pain." Hurt can be a great teacher. Of course, one protects his child from the devastating loss and from the crippling hurt, but it is a myth to believe that anytime one can protect his child from pain, he should.

6. *Only the young and hip can communicate with the young and hip.* This myth suggests that only those who know the jargon and the rhetoric of teenagers can effectively communicate with them. If this were true, parents would be excluded from effective communication with their children. This is a myth. Some very effective youth ministers and youth workers are older persons who are not connected to the youth culture in terms of the way they dress, the way they talk, or the music they listen to. You do not have to look like a Christian rock star to minister effectively to young people.

Most people who grew up in the church can remember a Sunday school teacher or youth worker who knew nothing about the youth culture of their era but effectively communicated the love of Christ to children and youth. While it is great to have an attractive young minister with a natural way of interacting with teenagers and see this person make a difference in their lives, it is erroneous to think that it is necessary to be young and hip to be effective ministers or successful parents.

The Principle of Nurture Versus Control

There is a powerful concept from the literature of psychology that can help one understand the important relationship of nurture and control. Schaefer's Circumplex Model gives valuable insight in ministering the grace of God to young people, especially to children in one's own family. Most relationships with children, Schaefer suggests, is some combination of nurture and control. He defines nurture as "expressions of love, expressions of acceptance, and expressions of care—the nurturing, loving, caring quality children receive." On the other hand, control is "delivering the bad news to children." It is telling them what they cannot do when they do not want to hear it. It is imposing a control over their lives—delivering the "thou shalts" and the "thou shalt nots."

Schaefer maintains that the higher the level of nurture given the child, the higher the level of control that can be given the child and still have a healthy relationship. In studying family environments, his research showed that if he divided young people by grouping into (1) a high-nurture, high-control group, (2) a low-nurture, low-control group, (3) a high-nurture, low-control group, and (4) a low-nurture, high-control group, distinct patterns appeared.

A high-nurturing, high-controlling parent is one who, along with much love, gives a great deal of structure, rules, and direction, thus imposing a high level of discipline. A high-nurturing parent, who gives lots of love and unconditional acceptance can impose more discipline without resentment. In all of his research, Schaefer found that the best adjusted children are those whose parents gave them high nurture and high control. His models show that if one wants to give a child high levels of control, he must give the child a great deal of nurture. On the other end of the scale, the children most often found in criminal situations, addicted to drugs or alcohol and having inappropriate social adjustment, are children whose parents gave them high control and low nurture. Somewhere in the middle are children from the low-nurture, low-control environments or high-nurture, low-control environments.

What Schaefer is basically saying is that one can discipline his children as much as he should as long as he also shows them love. Not just love them; show them love. Demonstrate nurture, and one can demonstrate control. In the same way, working with young people in a group, one can be controlling if one is also loving and caring. One can impose rules, structure, and a great deal of discipline, if one also brings acceptance, nurture, and a great deal of love. Schaefer's work has been replicated in many populations with similar results. If one will love a lot, he can discipline a lot and have a very healthy outcome. But if he disciplines without loving, he is going to have a negative outcome.

This is what Christ demonstrated. Jesus was high nurture, high control. He is the model to parents for their children. Jesus Christ never offered an example of no rules, no limits, no structure, and no expectations. He did have rules. He did have discipline. He does have expectations. At the same time, however, He constantly, in ways far more profound and eloquent than just words, conveys this message to everyone: "I love you. I care for you. I show you my love."

> I have talked to parents who believe in being really tough on their kids. They offer the church as an example and say, "You've got to give them discipline, you've got to give them structure, you've got to give them rules. After all, God gives that. God has rules. God has structure. God has discipline." And I remind myself that God did indeed have rules, but He also had so much love that He died for them. He can ask

a lot, because He gave a lot. I ask these questions of all who are in ministry. If you expect a lot, do you give a lot? If you want to impose the rules, do you also show love? If we are going to express the demands of God, will we also take the time to express our great love in small ways and in large ways, over and over, for a lifetime? As ministers, we must learn how to make family life work in the midst of the demands of the ministry. May God give us the grace to do that every day.

13 GUIDELINES FOR PERSONAL PRODUCTIVITY: PART ONE

By Paul Conn, Ph.D.

Ask any group of normal adults to consider what they wish they could accomplish in life, or ask them what they would like for psychology to bring to them, and their responses could be placed into these two categories: how to be happy and how to be productive. Most psychological, emotional, and spiritual needs flow from a desire to find happiness, which include a desire to love, to be loved, and to meet self-esteem needs. One important aspect to finding happiness is to be productive. However, it is not just happiness that is desired, but to be fruitful, to matter, to make a difference, and to find meaning in productivity. One wants to do good work and have others recognize their good work.

No matter how much fun people have, or how much entertainment or recreation they experience, usually people are not happy unless they are productive. A minister studies to be a more effective minister, because fruitfulness in ministry is a key to happiness. This is really a catch-22 situation.

People want to be happy, but cannot be happy until they are productive. Productivity comes first. This means that productivity must be defined in broader terms than reaching one's ultimate goal. Productivity is a part of the journey, as well as the destination. Preparing for the task can be some of the most productive times in life. When the ground is being plowed, or the seed being sown, that is as important as reaping, because there can be no harvest without preparation, cultivation, and sowing.

This desire for happiness and productivity has been tapped by the popular psychology of the last 25 years. The bookshelves are crowded with titles on how to manage one's life, how to manage one's friendships, how to manage time, how to cope with depression, and how to have significant relationships with other people. The publishing phenomenon of the last quarter century has been the proliferation of self-help books. In these books, popular psychology has drawn from the serious psychological literature of the last century to address the vital topics of being happy and being productive.

The Scripture speaks to the issue of productivity. "This is to my Father's glory, that you bear much fruit, showing yourselves to be my disciples" (John 15:8 NIV). Jesus teaches that to be productive or fruitful is to glorify God and demonstrate discipleship. Christ is obviously interested in the believer's personal piety, in the cleanness of his life, and in the degree to which he lives according to the principles of holiness. He is interested in the believer's study of His Word, his communication with Him, and his worship. But in this passage of Scripture, as clearly as in any other single Scripture, Jesus teaches that being good is not enough. He wants one to be more than just good and more than just dedicated; He wants him to be fruitful and productive.

There are principles for fruitful and productive living that are drawn from a vast range of experiments, research, and writings in the literature of psychology. These, along with Scripture and common sense, give valuable guidelines for productive living. First, note this caveat—success is not the same as productivity. Success is measured in terms of how much money one makes, what position one has in life, what degree has been earned, or how people evaluate one's accomplishments. The world regards these as success, but that is not what productivity in the spiritual life is about. The productivity characterized by the spiritual is defined only by accomplishment in things related to the work of the Kingdom. The following principles taken from the literature of psychology give insight on how to be a more fruitful and productive person in this dimension.

Ten Principles for Productive People

1. *Productive people accept the pressure of chronic discontent.* Productive people are willing to be somewhat chronically dissatisfied. In a productive ministry, one continually feels the pressure of not being able to do enough or to get it exactly right. Productive people have to accept this pressure and not walk away from it. This means living with chronic discontent—what can be described as a holy or a righteous discontent. Believing that God can help make things better becomes the fuel for production. It is much easier to lower one's standards in life and to settle for lower levels of produc-

tivity, but in any situation where one is perfectly happy with the way things are, nothing is likely to change.

The size of a church is not the only measure of productivity. However, if one has a church with 50 people and feels happy about it, there is little incentive to do the small things that would take the church up to 60 people. On the other hand, the pastor of a 50-member church who would like to see twice as many people in the pews receiving God's grace has a discontent that fuels productivity. That is the mark of one who has a willingness to never be truly at ease in Zion. There is a fine line here in terms of the mental health of the minister. Obviously, God does not want one to be perpetually frustrated in His work and experience debilitating bouts of stress and depression. He does, however, want the minister to always be open to the vision and the better things He has for him.

Another caveat needs to be inserted here. Discontent should not be based on a comparison with others. Think about the areas of life with which there is discontent. If those areas of discontent are drawn from a comparison with what other people have or do not have, that is not a holy discontent. That is a human discontent, maybe even a carnal discontent. Carnal discontent will not make one more productive. It will just make one more miserable. God never challenges an individual to be chronically miserable—to be a complainer or whiner. Furthermore, God never challenges one to do as much as another person, or have as much as another person. There is something very poisonous about constant comparisons with others. In the Christian life, the focus is on Jesus. The focus that gives rise to discontent should never be a comparison of what one has or does, or with what others have or do. Discontent is based on a comparison of what an individual's ministry is at any point in time as it relates to the vision God has given him.

2. *Productive people have specific visions.* Many unproductive people have visions, but productive people have specificity in their visions. Productive people translate their visions into specific steps, behaviors, and goals so their work accomplishes their visions. A vision, in and of itself, especially if it is grand and diffused, does not assure productivity. Visions generate productivity when two things happen. First, when they are made specific, and second, when they are connected to specific behavior. Should one's vision be for an enlarged opportunity to preach, specific steps must be taken, such as creating flyers that center on one's strengths, and actively seeking appointments. This is accomplished by writing letters, by making telephone calls, and by making personal contacts. If an individual is a youth pastor with a vision of having the young people in his youth group introduced to community service, he should devise specific ways to get them to serve. If the vision is to have a youth group that is serving other people, that is a wonderful, biblical vision. But for it to be a productive vision, one must take the next step. Ask the hard question: What specifically would a youth group that is committed to Christian service be doing? What would be its schedule? What particular activities would it engage in? Instead of just praying, *God, make my young people productive, help them to get involved, give them a heart for service, and give them a heart for ministry,* one should de-

vise a specific vision with a single measurable part of what a youth group like that would do. The second step is to determine what one should do to implement that vision.

> When I became president at Lee University, I had many visions of what I thought God wanted to do here at Lee. My first vision was for an improved campus. I knew we were far from having what we needed to be able to serve people well. For a few months, I walked around the campus praying for God to bless us and make us more effective and productive. Finally, I had to get to the point of identifying specifically the components of my first vision of an improved campus. I settled on one old building on our campus that was empty, out of use, and full of asbestos. The old library building had been abandoned because the new library had been built, and the old one sat empty in the middle of the campus. So when my vision became specific, I quit praying for a better campus and started praying for money to renovate the old library building. With this, I moved in the direction of a more productive ministry. Then, I had to go to the hardest step. I had to get into the habit of deciding what I would do each day that would move us closer to the implementation of the vision. That's the tough part, but that's how productive people merge their vision with the Lord's work.

3. *Productive people fast before feasting.* Work first and celebrate later. Productive people know how to delay gratification. Delay of gratification is a biblical principle which simply says that to be productive and to be effective, one has to wait for some things he really wants and, in the meantime, do some things that he really does not want to do.

Life has to be endured to be enjoyed. Nonproductive people want to reverse this process.

Hedonism, a philosophy of the secular world, says "eat, drink, and be merry, for tomorrow you may die." That philosophy is expressed in an approach to life that says, "first the feast, then the hangover." Or, "enjoy yourself as much as you can, and live with the consequences later." However, God's principle of happy and productive living is "first the fast, then the feast." First give the effort, the sweat, the strain, then comes the payoff. First, comes the work, then the reward.

Scott Peck, a psychiatrist from the state of New York, presents a helpful concept. He calls it scheduling the pain. What he means by that is that there is a certain amount of pain in life. No human being can avoid the pain, but one can schedule the pain. By scheduling the pain, he means experience the pain early, instead of late. Handling dental problems presents an example. A person gets a few small cavities, and instead of going to the dentist, he delays the dental work and the pain associated with a visit to the dentist. This individual has just scheduled the pain for later. Without the dental work, he will experience tooth decay and then have to go to the dentist with a more serious and more painful problem. Scott Peck says that pain which is scheduled late is more severe than pain which is scheduled early. Not only that, the individual has been worrying about the pain that he knows he is going to have later on. Peck says scheduling the pain early means that when the dental problem first arises, one should go to the dentist and accept the pain early. Face it, and get the problem solved.

There is no achievement in the ministry that occurs without pain. This means hard work, sacrifice, deprivation—things one would like to avoid. All productive ministers and pastors have embraced pain in ministry. This principle of "first the fast, and then the feast" says if one will do what he would rather not do early, he will be able to achieve what he wants to achieve later in the kingdom of God. That is the purpose of education. There are more pleasurable things to do with one's life than studying, even things that would seem to be more productive; however, fruitfulness demands preparation and cultivation.

Vince Lombardi, the great football coach of the Green Bay Packers once said that his job was to get grown men to do things that they hated in order to achieve what they had always dreamed of accomplishing. In the hot sun of the late summer training camp when there were no games to play—just training, conditioning, and drills—Lombardi convinced men that if they would endure the pain of preparation, they would wear the championship ring of victory.

This is what Christ would say: " I want you to do the things you do not want to do, early, so you can have the experience of a dream of a lifetime, later." When a minister does the things necessary for development—makes the calls, studies, prays, develops relationships—in the early stages of ministry, that is "the fast." Not much enjoyment is experienced, just a lot of tough times. Then comes "the feast"—a time of reward. Sow, then reap. Fast, then feast is a biblical principle for fruitfulness and productiveness.

4. *Productive people tell themselves good news.* They understand the biblical perspective on the value of a positive thought life. "Whatever things are true, whatever things are noble, whatever things are just, whatever things are pure, whatever things are lovely, whatever things are of a good report . . . [think] on these things" (Philippians 4:8 NKJV). In the Old and New Testaments, the Bible teaches that one's thought life matters. "As [a man] thinketh in his heart, so is he" (Proverbs 23:7). The passage in Philippians 4:8 implies that one should ignore the things that are ugly and bad. Do not deny them or lie about whether they exist, just ignore them and refuse to dwell on the negative. There are unpleasant realities and only an idiot would deny the presence of adversity in life. One plans a big service for months, expecting several hundred people, and a dozen people and a dog show up. Do not engage in some sort of a silly, charismatic, happy talk. Just admit it was a disaster, and go on. Acknowledge the bad news. Accept the failure. Call it what it is, but do not dwell on it. Rather, let the things that are positive and good control the thinking processes.

5. *Productive people hold themselves accountable.* They take responsibility for results and outcomes. They understand that what they do makes the difference. Spiritual outcomes are in the hands of God, but before the spiritual outcomes are apparent, many nonspiritual outcomes exist. These are the logistical elements of one's work. The productive Christian accepts responsibility for these outcomes, and leaves the spiritual results to God.

When a minister delivers a sermon, he has no control over how people respond to that sermon, spiritually. Present a message calling for repentance, and the minister has no control over whether people come forward and accept the plan of salvation. Since he has no control over it, he is not responsible for it. The Holy Spirit convicts people, and they are responsible for their reactions to the gospel. But there are some things for which the minister is responsible. He is accountable for the level of sermon preparation that he brings to the pulpit. If the sound system is bad and distracts from the message, he is accountable. If the piano is out of tune and ruins the music, he is responsible for having it tuned. If the church bulletin is badly written and poorly printed, he is accountable for improving the quality of the bulletin.

Nonproductive Christians and ministers seem to see everything as being in God's hands and suggest that, if it is God's will, it will turn out right, if it is not God's will, it won't. They leave it all to God. That is a just another way of avoiding accountability and responsibility for their part of the equation. God is sovereign, but productive ministers hold themselves accountable for everything within their control. They know they are accountable for the actual quality and product of their work. Productive people hold themselves responsible for everything leading to the moment when God takes over and, by his Holy Spirit, achieves the results.

If one is going to be a fruitful minister, living for the glory of God and showing himself to be His disciple, he will hold himself accountable for all the aspects of ministry over which he has control. Then he will let go, turn it loose, and relinquish his work into the hands of God. After one does all that can be done, he should give that labor to the Lord because it is, after all, really His work, and only He can produce the final spiritual results.

14 GUIDELINES FOR PERSONAL PRODUCTIVITY: PART TWO

By Paul Conn, Ph.D.

The two foundation stones of life are personal happiness and personal productivity. God is interested in both aspects of life, because He knows that it is difficult to be happy for a long period of time without being productive. Men and women were created that way—to want to matter, to find meaning in what they do. This chapter continues a discussion of the principles of personal productivity in ministry. Five of those principles were presented in the last chapter.

Ten Principles for Productive People

6. *Productive people ignore unfair criticism.* If one is doing the work of the Kingdom, he is going to be criticized. Productive people expect it, and they ignore it. Their role model is Christ. Jesus received a constant barrage of criticism throughout His ministry from a wide variety of people. Since productive people march to a different drummer, they are frequently misunderstood. Pursuit of the vision God

has given may cause one to rub people the wrong way from time to time. At times one may be ignored, discounted, brushed aside, and marginalized, that is, put on the margins of society. One may even be written off as being not very sophisticated, not very smart, or simply being misguided. However, even in the best of all circumstances, where one does everything right, many people still will not understand and will not speak well of the believer's accomplishments.

> For many years I have worked as a free-lance writer and have written books with several well-known people. One of them was Johnny Cash. I spent a lot of time with Johnny Cash, and on one occasion heard a friend of his, who was an agent and knew the industry very well, respond to criticism of Cash. He said, "Johnny Cash is so honest and so straight that it constantly brings him into conflict with an industry that's built on hype and exaggeration." The kernel of truth in there is that if one lives in a world built on hype and exaggeration and is always totally honest, that candor and honesty will bring him into conflict.

If, in a world drunk on personal pleasure and self-gratification, one calls that kind of life sinful and points out that there is a better way to live than the pursuit of personal pleasure, that message will bring criticism and conflict. This conflict is not bad. A certain amount of criticism can be a good indicator that maybe one is doing the right thing.

Of all these principles, this one can be most easily abused. Knowing they take a controversial stance, however, does not give people a license to be jerks with a lack of social grace as if to say, "I'm God's man doing God's plan and who cares if people criticize me." It is unthinkable to hide behind a moral position to become abusive and obnoxious. However, there is a strong principle both in Scripture and in psychology that productive people frequently cut against the grain of less productive people. Their dreams will be beyond the dreams of normal people, their self-confidence will be misunderstood, and their discontent will be unsettling. So, they draw criticism.

Jesus was criticized because He ate with sinners. His critics took it a step further, claiming He was a glutton and drank too much. If Jesus had been in a damage-control mode as many ministers are, it would have been very easy for Him to say, "If I go to dinner with sinners who are overeating and drinking, even though I am not, it will still have negative implications for My ministry, so, I'll just stay away." Jesus did not take that approach, because Jesus expected unfair criticism and ignored it. For Him to constantly be in a damage-control posture would have required Him to shrink His interaction with people and pull back so sharply that He would have been unable to meet the challenges of His ministry and fulfill the mission for which He came. Jesus came to seek out the lost, and to do that, took Him into the company of sinners. For that, He was brutally and unfairly criticized. How did Jesus respond? He did not respond by scaling down His ministry to avoid criticism. He expected unfair criticism and ignored it. He was accused of breaking the Sabbath laws and other Jewish laws. Sometimes, He was guilty and at other times He was not guilty, but He was oblivious to the attacks.

The higher purpose of Jesus Christ shielded Him from the damage of the criticism. Productive people will be hard on themselves in the small things. They will make sure that they do not abuse their callings, but then when criticism comes for the things they do in good faith, in good conscience, in the execution of their ministries and their callings, they simply shrug off the criticisms.

Another aspect of abuse is not criticism for something one might do, but a belittling of one's dreams and vision. Productive people believe in what they are going to achieve for the Lord before it is apparent that they can achieve it. This always brings pressure. A tension exists between what a truly effective minister can sense in his spirit is going to occur through his ministry and what other people can see. People can deal a crushing blow when they belittle one's dreams, sometimes not even meaning to be hostile or nasty. They may just give a kind of sarcastic knowing smile when one starts to talk about the great things he thinks that God can do through him and his ministry. This will never hurt unless that individual lets that knowing smile steal his dreams.

7. *Productive people keep a tight focus.* Productive people are not easily distracted from the basic core of their work. To be fruitful in the kingdom of God, it is necessary to find a central theme for God's work in one's life, focus on it, and not be distracted from fulfilling that vision. The ability of a man or a woman to get a single-minded, godly purpose generates tremendous power. To take a fully focused individual and bring the power of the Holy Spirit and the grace of Jesus Christ to that focus is a great place to begin a mighty work for the Lord.

But it is a hard thing to do because distractions are numerous.

Highly effective people understand they cannot do everything, so they focus on the basic theme or core of God's work in their lives. They are willing to peel away from their lives those things that drain off time and energy from that primary theme. People who are in this mode can be very tedious. They get on one's nerves, because they tend to be single-minded and talk about the same thing all the time. Highly effective people might be described as obsessive. Saint Paul certainly was. Read the writings of the apostle, and it is obvious that he constantly talks about forgetting those things that are in the past, looking forward to the things which lie ahead, and pressing toward a mark with single-minded focus and purpose (see Philippians 3:13, 14). Productive ministers settle on a few things that God wants them to do, and then they tighten the focus.

Take a small magnifying glass and focus the energy of the sun on leaves, twigs, or paper, and they will burst into flames. Where did the power to ignite come from? It came from the sun, but that same power was already there. The individual did not generate any more sun power when he put the magnifying glass over the leaves and twigs. He took the sun power that was already available over a wide area and focused it on a single point. By bringing the sun's energy together in a concentrated single point, he gained the power to ignite something, not just to warm it. Within one's vast potential, one already has in his grasp the skills he needs, the energy he needs, and the resources he needs, unless his efforts are spread over such a wide area that his focus is defused and his energy is dissipated. There is value in laying aside peripheral projects to gain power with concentration and focus.

> I have a friend who grew up on the Western plains where there were very few trees. He moved to the Pacific Northwest where there were huge, beautiful trees and secured a site to build a house. He told the architects not to cut down a single tree. He said, "I want you to place the house on this lot so it won't be necessary to cut down a single tree, because I love these trees, and it would just be a shame to lose any of them." The builder and the architect went to the building site and spent hours looking over the possibilities. Finally, the architect came back to my friend and said, "I hate to tell you this, but if you want to build this house on that lot, some of these trees have to go."

That is how the believer's life is. There is nothing wrong with the trees; they are beautiful. But when God's calling takes first place in one's life, something has to go. It might be a personal pleasure, a type of entertainment, a hobby, a relationship, or something that is loved, but just realize that one cannot have everything. Choices have to be made. A powerful principle of productivity in the kingdom of God is that God is looking for men and women who will get focused, stop trying to live their lives all over the lot, and be willing to give up some things to concentrate their energies on God's calling.

It is all a matter of staying on message. When Bill Clinton ran for President in 1992, George Bush was a huge favorite to win. Clinton won with a message focused on the economy. A sign in the National

Democratic Headquarters had one message that simply said, "It's the economy, stupid." The challenge was to stay on message. The campaign staff met with Clinton every morning to keep Clinton focused because he liked to talk about all kinds of things. He liked to talk about foreign affairs, education and a myriad of subjects, but their polling had shown them that the public wanted to hear about the economy, and the reason they would vote for Clinton over Bush was because they thought Clinton would do a better job with the economy. Once they found the message, they stayed on it. Not schools, not the military, not foreign affairs, not transportation and housing, it was the economy. That single-mindedness, more than any other factor, won Clinton the victory. His handlers understood the power of a focused message.

The ministry of Jesus certainly had the quality of focus. In fact, Jesus stayed on message. He understood what He was here to do. People tried to draw Him into politics, but He was not interested in politics. People wanted to draw Him into different kinds of things, but He would only be what He came to earth to be, and would only do what He came to do. From the day He was born to the Virgin Mary, to the day He ascended to heaven, the central theme in His ministry was to redeem all of mankind through His personal sacrifice and to leave behind a small group of people who would spread that good news. He was never deflected from that theme. Every productive minister will follow that principle.

8. *Productive people find and join a conspiracy of mutual support.* Bill Mitchell, a K-12 educator and public school superintendent, writes about the value of sharing and cooperation in schools. He

uses this phrase "a conspiracy of mutual support" to talk about ways in which one finds allies in life. Ministers need to find people who will believe in them and team with them in a mutual conspiracy for good works. They conspire to believe in one another, to stand against people who are unfairly critical, to support one another's dreams, and fulfill one another's visions. In this conspiracy of mutual sup- port, people matter to one another. Sorrows and joys are shared.

Productive people do not have to cut themselves off from others to do God's work. To the contrary, one of the things they need to keep them fruitful in His kingdom is a support group, a set of friends, a family, or a network of people with whom they collaborate. Sometimes, it may be a strong marriage in which there is real sharing and warmth. But if one wants to be productive and effective in the kingdom of God, he should not fail to develop a small circle in which he can be himself—in which he can share, trust, and be trusted. In the ministry, that can sometimes be hard to find, but it is a key to doing God's work effectively. Productive people have friends who believe in them.

9. *Productive people don't sweat the small stuff.* This is another way of saying keep the "big stuff" in mind. This does not mean ignore the details. It means to keep clearly in mind what one is really working for—the big picture, not the little picture. It is an irony, almost a paradox. Productive and fruitful people are able simultaneously to keep in their minds the large dimensions of what they are doing for God, while at the same time, not be so carried away with the grand design that they fail to do the little things. It is a balancing act, and

the principle simply says, "keep the big picture in mind." No matter how committed one is to the Lord, he is still human and will, on occasion, grow tired and weary in spirit. In order to combat that, the primary thing one must do is keep the big picture in mind. One must remember who he is working for and what he is working for.

When a woman is expecting a baby for the first time, she is constantly looking forward to that baby, buying little clothes, knitting little booties, and thinking about a name. For much of the time, pregnancy may not be pleasant and can become a very negative experience if the expectant mother focuses on the little discomforts, how she looks, and how awkward she feels in the late stages of pregnancy. But watch these young mothers as they look forward to the arrival of their babies. Their focus is not on the third or fourth month fetus or the morning sickness, they remain focused on the baby. From the very first day the young woman knows that she is going to have a baby, her mind fast forwards to the end with a baby in her arms or in the little bassinet. She knows that the discomfort is temporary and what is going to happen in a few months will be worth the temporary distress. Do not think about that intermediate stage, focus on the final product. That is how one must be with the things of God. It may take a long, slow, sometimes unpleasant, incubation period for the things of God to be done through one's ministry. One could indeed get very discouraged and come to hate the privations and sacrifices if he does not keep the final product in mind.

> I really believe in the power of God to change the lives of students at Lee University. We have

> Lee Day here in the spring to welcome high school students and tell them about our university. I remember a few years ago on Lee Day, it was hot, we were crowded, people had problems, and I was running around helping anyone I could. Some state group came in, and there was no ice for their soft drinks. So, I drove to the 7-11 and got a bag of crushed ice, came back, put ice in cups, and served cokes to these teenagers, who didn't seem to really want to do anything but grab a coke and run off to have a good time. That day I got focused on the little stuff. I'm thinking, *Here I am in my mid-40s. I've trained long and hard. I've committed my life to ministry, and look what I'm doing—pouring cokes for teenagers.* It wasn't particularly uplifting. I went home still fretting and focused on how trivial life can be. Late that night, I received a telephone call from a friend who was a pastor and in a state several hundred miles away. He said, "I just had to tell you this. Our daughter, who is on campus for Lee Day, just called us. We have been praying she would go to Lee. However, she has never had any interest in going to Lee, but she called to say that she felt that the Lord wanted her to attend college at Lee University." That young woman came to Lee, and I kept my eye on her. She is now a wonderful Christian woman who graduated a year or so ago. That is the big picture, and it taught me a lesson. There is going to be a lot of small, tedious stuff in my life, but if I don't sweat the small stuff and keep my eye on the big picture, I'm going to be fruitful.

10. *Productive people take time to recharge the battery, get some rest, and enjoy the trip.* God does not want the believer's life to be all drudgery, all obsessive focus, all work. God engineered mankind to need rest, to relax, and to have recreation. No

part of one's job is so important that God wants one to destroy his health to achieve it. No task on the to-do list in one's ministry is so important that God wants him to neglect his family and be alienated from them. Productive people in the kingdom of God work hard, care deeply, and hold themselves fiercely responsible for being the best they can be, but they also take time to "smell the roses," revel in wholesome pleasures, and fully enjoy life. That is what God wants for everyone.

APPENDICES

GLOSSARY

GLOSSARY

(This glossary relates only to those words deemed not to be in common usage or words having a unique meaning in the context of these lessons. Terms already defined in the text are not included in this glossary.)

1. **advocacy**—the act or process of supporting a cause or proposal

2. **autonomy**—the quality or state of being self-governing, especially the right of self-government. For the child, autonomy relates to the control of bodily functions.

3. **catharsis**—purification; cleansing; psychologically, catharsis relates to an emptying of frustration and stress.

4. **cognitive**—based on cognition—the act or process of knowing, including both awareness and judgments

5. **congruent**—the quality or state of agreeing; where actions and feelings are in agreement

6. **contextualism**—related to the surroundings; environment; setting

7. **depression**—an extreme state of sadness accompanied by difficulty in thinking and a lowering of vitality and functional activity

8. **deviation**—noticeable or marked departure from accepted norms of behavior

9. **dispositional**—prevailing tendency, mood, or inclination; the tendency of something to act in a certain manner under given circumstances

10. **egocentric**—self-centered; selfish

11. **free-floating anxiety**—felt as an emotion that arises, producing stress without apparent cause

12. **generativity**—transitions of the generations; midlife transition

13. **ideology**—visionary theorizing; a systematic body of concepts, especially about human life or culture

14. **identity**—the distinguishing character or personality of an individual; the relation established by psychological identification

15. **industry**—steady or habitual effort; a systematic labor for some useful purpose

16. **inferiority**—a feeling that one is of little or less importance, value, or merit

17. **initiative**—related to taking control, introducing action at one's own discretion

18. **integrity**—firm adherence to a code of moral values; incorruptibility; honesty

19. **nonnormative**—lacking the usual norms

20. **normative**—of, relating to, or determining norms or standards conforming to or based on norms

21. **perception**—observation; a mental image; concept

22. **pragmatic**—practical as opposed to idealistic; relating to matters of fact or practical affairs, often to the exclusion of intellectual or artistic matters

23. **psychosexual**—of or relating to the mental, emotional, and behavioral aspects of sexual development or emotional attitudes concerning sexual activity

24. **psychosocial**—relating both psychological and social aspects; relating social conditions to mental health

25. **psychosomatic**—of, relating to, concerned with, or involving both mind and body; concerned with bodily symptoms caused by mental or emotional disturbance

26. **tantamount**—equivalent in value, significance, or effect

27. **transcendent**—exceeding usual limits; surpassing; being beyond comprehension

BIBLIOGRAPHY

BIBLIOGRAPHY

Collins, Gary. *Effective Counseling.* Carol Stream, IL: Creation House, 1976.

Davids, Anthony and Trygg Engen. *Introductory Psychology.* New York: Random House, 1975.

Erikson, Erik. *Childhood and Society.* New York: Norton, 1963.

---. *Identity: Youth and Crisis.* New York: Norton, 1968.

Frankl, Viktor. *Man's Search for Meaning.* Boston: Beacon Press, 1939.

Freud, Sigmund. *The Interpretation of Dreams.* New York: Basic Books, 1900.

---. *Psychopathology of Everyday Life.* New York: Norton, 1901.

Gilliland, Burl and Richard James. *Theories and Strategies in Counseling and Psychotherapy.* 4th ed., Boston: Allyn and Bacon, 1998.

Jung, Carl. *The Undiscovered Self.* Boston: Little, Brown, 1957.

Kubler-Ross, Elisabeth. *On Death and Dying.* New York: Simon & Schuster, rpt. 1997.

Leman, Kevin. *Bringing Up Kids Without Tearing Them Down: How to Raise Confident, Successful Children.* New York: Thomas Nelson, 1995.

Maslow, Abraham. *Motivation and Personality.* New York: Harper and Row, 1970.

Okun, Barbara. *Effective Helping: Interviewing and Counseling Techniques.* 5th ed., Pacific Grove, CA: Brooks/Cole Publishing Co., 1997.

Peck, M. Scott. *The Road Less Traveled: A New Psychology of Love, Traditional Values, Spiritual Growth.* New York: Simon & Schuster, 1978.

Piaget, J. *The Origins of Intelligence in Children.* New York: International Universities Press, 1952.

Rogers, Carl. *Client-Centered Therapy.* Boston: Houghton Mifflin, 1951.

Rousseau, Jean-Jacques. *Emile.* Rutland: Charles E. Tuttle Co., Inc., reissued, 1992.

Schaefer, Earl S. "A Circumplex Model for Maternal Behavior." *Journal of Abnormal and Social Psychoogy.* rpt. in *Bobbs-Merrill Reprint Series of the Social Sciences.* Indianapolis: Bobbs-Merrill, 1966.

Skinner, B.F. *About Behaviorism.* New York: Knopf, 1974.

---. *Science and Human Behavior.* New York: MacMillan, 1953.